Beams of Light

*A wealth of spiritual insights
sure to brighten your day*

J Douglas Bottorff

Copyright © 2016 J Douglas Bottorff

All rights reserved.

ISBN: 1533198330
ISBN-13: 978-1533198334

Acknowledgments

Unless otherwise noted, all biblical citations are taken from the "Revised Standard Version of the Bible, copyright 1952 [2nd edition, 1971] by the Division of Christian Education of the National Council of the Churches of Christ in the United States of America. Used by permission. All rights reserved."

Cover Photo: Rod Waddington. Photo has been cropped to accommodate cover design.

Contents

Introduction	i
This Battle is Not Yours	1
Plowing New Ground	3
Strength in the Face of Fear	5
A Message from Clutter	7
Doing and Being	9
Trying to Love	**11**
Give Yourself to Love	12
The White Stone	14
New Beginnings	16
Recognize Your Good	18
Travelers Through Eternity	20
Refuse to Quit	22
God, the Creative Life Force	24
Spiritual Enlightenment Revisited	26
The Emerging Soul	28
The Mythology of Love	30
The Nearness of God	32
From the Inside Out	34
The Forgiveness Principle	36
Understanding Oneness	38
The Light of Compassion	**40**
The Power of Perseverance	41
The Wellspring of Good	43

The Scope of Life 45
The Tie that Binds 47
Consciousness 49
The Paradigm of Oneness 51
The Paradigm of Oneness 52
Who Am I? 54
Oneness, What it Means 56
Soul Evolution: Fact or Fiction? 58
The Healing Principle 60
The Consciousness Factor 62
The Choice is Yours 64
Praying for Others 66
The Attitude of Gratitude 68
The Call from Home 70
The Prayer Principle 72
Soul, Consciousness and Body 74
Going Alone 75
I Am the Vine 77
Releasing Loved Ones 79
Your Divine Core 81
Making God Yours 83
The Quest for Freedom 85
Soul Recovery 87
The Freedom You Seek 89
The Everlasting Arms 91
Our Spiritual Home 93

The Narrow Gate of Meditation 94
The Prayer Dynamic.. 96
Victory in Silence 98
Peace, be Still 100
The Gift of Uncertainty 102
Yes and No 104
Your Inner Teacher 106
The Lord's Prayer Series 108
Open Your Mind 109
The Expansive Action of God 111
The Prospering act of Forgiveness 113
Freedom in Forgiveness 115
The Tempter Within 117
One Presence, One Power 119
The Lord's Prayer 121
A Quantum Leap of Faith 122
Demonstrating Prosperity 124
A Question of Faith 126
Beyond the Dark Night of the Soul 128
Let There be Light 130
Choosing Your Vision 132
One Source 134
Giving Up Means Giving Way 136
What is Greater Good? 138
How to Let Go 140
Guidance 142

Run To, Not From 143
Living Your Truth 145
Seeing is Believing 147
The Invincible Spirit 149
The Faith Factor 151
The Intuitive Voice 153
The Storm Will Pass 155
Navigating Through Illusion 157
Losing and Living? 159
In Harmony with God 161
The Whole Picture 162
The Forgiveness Dynamic 164
The False Prophet 166
This Too Shall Pass 169
Letting Go of the Old 171
Who is in Charge? 173
The Call 174
Transcending the Law of Karma 176
Events and Experience 178
View From the Rim 180
What You See is What You Get 182
What's in Your House? 184
When Doors Close, Minds Open 186
The Twenty-Third Psalm Series 188
The Lord is My Shepherd 189
Beside Still Waters 191

The Path of Righteousness 193

Finding Peace in the Valley 195

My Cup Overflows 197

Dwelling in the House of the Lord 199

Facts versus Truth 201

An Inlet and Outlet 202

Filling Your Life Right Where You Are 204

Forgiveness and the Art of Letting Go 206

Focus Your Energy 208

Misguided Guidance 210

For This You Were Born 212

Freedom in Divine Order 214

From Place to Process 216

A Better Solution 218

God Mind, Human Thinking 219

How to Ask God for Help 221

Roles and Purpose 223

Singleness of Purpose 225

The Missing Thing 227

The Personal and Transcendent Aspects of God 229

The Secret of Change 231

The Key to Power 233

The Prospering Law of Giving 235

The Spiritual Context 237

The Thrones of Angels 239

A Perceptual Lens 241

Understanding Grace 242

What's in a Name? 244

When Tough Love is Called For 246

Where is Your Heart? 248

Why Am I Here? 250

You Just Know 252

The Theory of Everything 254

Your Spiritual Guide 256

About the Author 258

Introduction

Beams of Light is a collection of over a hundred short and powerful inspirational messages that cover a wide range of subjects important to the spiritual seeker today. Each message raises a common issue and offers a sound application of easily grasped spiritual principles.

The more we give our light to the world, the more we realize that we already dwell in the house of the Lord. Being a conscious giver opens our eyes to things we cannot see when we are drawn in upon ourselves. The world becomes a brighter place because we bring the needed light of compassion.

We are spiritual beings who have, for reasons we know at the deepest level, stepped into this earthly experience to accomplish some work important to us. We brought with us our connection to our eternal source of guidance and supply, a resource of wisdom and guidance that will always lead us to the right answers when we need them.

There may be a better solution to our need than the one we envision. We could be looking for a specific change in circumstances when all that is needed is a slight shift in attitude.

Our consciousness is a kind of lens through which we view everything. If we hold onto ideas that are out of integrity with the nature of the soul, we hinder the fuller expression of its true essence.

Spiritual growth is the process of bringing our consciousness, the sum of our beliefs, into alignment with what is true of us at the deepest level.

Within these pages, you are sure to find insights that will affirm your convictions and challenge you to consider new ways of seeing yourself and your world.

This Battle is Not Yours

Do not fear or be dismayed at this great multitude; for the battle is not yours but God's.

2 Chronicles 20:15

Everyone has moments of uncertainty, of trial, of self doubt and even despair. In these moments we seek help from all kinds of sources. We'll turn to books, counselors, ministers, doctors, friends or family members. Any one of these may pass on some level of assurance that things are going to work out, that harmony will be restored in our body or in our affairs. With this bit of assurance, we rest a little easier, regain some of our optimism and turn our attention to more creative endeavors.

It is a freeing thought to realize that the strength we seem to draw from others is really a process of opening our minds to our own deeper resource. In consciously returning to this inner resource, we find the battle is not ours, that the great harmonizing power of God working through us is bringing about a satisfying solution. In quietness and trust in this truth, the flame of new strength is kindled.

When you become consumed with a problem, you have simply relegated your attention to one miniscule aspect of your being. Your entire universe revolves around it. It is important to remember that there is nothing that can sever your connection with God. This limitless source of energy and inspiration lifts you out of even the apparently tightest corners. Regardless of how far you believe you have strayed from your center of power, God is still present and still flooding your being with the strength and assurance you need to move beyond this current stretch of uncertainty.

Begin now to know that whatever the challenge, whatever battle consumes your attention, it is not your battle but God's. Enter the peace of letting go of your frantic search for answers. Be still and trust that the answers you need are forthcoming. Turn from the apparent adversity and let new strength and courage rise from the core of your being.

This battle is not yours. Know that God is working through you in beautifully satisfying ways right now.

Plowing New Ground

> As they were going along the road, a man said to him, "I will follow you wherever you go." And Jesus said to him, "Foxes have holes, and birds of the air have nests; but the Son of man has nowhere to lay his head." To another he said, "Follow me." But he said, "Lord, let me first go and bury my father." But he said to him, "Leave the dead to bury their own dead; but as for you, go and proclaim the kingdom of God." Another said, "I will follow you, Lord; but let me first say farewell to those at my home." Jesus said to him, "No one who puts his hand to the plow and looks back is fit for the kingdom of God."
>
> Luke 9:57-62

This series of statements all point to the same issue: if you want to begin again, you must release your attachments to the past. This is not so much a call to let go of memories, fond or otherwise, but rather to stop using energy to continue to respond to these memories.

The only place we can effectively act is in the now moment. When we feel overburdened, it is because we are expending energy focusing on problems that are impossible to resolve in the present. All we can do is mull them over, dispersing our creative energy. It's like plowing the same furrow over and over. You can get just as exhausted plowing a single furrow a hundred times as plowing a hundred furrows once, and the result is much less satisfying.

Solutions to our challenges have a way of presenting themselves, though not necessarily on demand. We sometimes have to let situations mature to the point where we know exactly what to do. Our drain of energy comes from speculating on what should be done before it is possible to do it. Jesus advised letting the weeds and the crops grow together, refraining from pulling the weeds until they were clearly identifiable. There is much wisdom in this advice. How often do we destroy our present peace by focusing on eliminating weeds that remain out of our reach?

Today, take a moment to connect with your Source. Know that you have all the intelligence and energy necessary to do what is yours to do. If you feel overburdened, as if your life is going nowhere, know that you are re-plowing the same furrow. Let it go, and bring your energy into plowing new ground.

Strength in the Face of Fear

It doesn't take a brilliant metaphysician to point out the debilitating nature of fear. We've all experienced it. Because fear is always negative, we may not think of it as an energy that can work for us rather than against us. It is quite possible, in fact, to redirect this negative energy into creative action. I found this out while my wife and I were on a four day boat-camping trip on Lake Powell, in Utah.

One afternoon, we were hit with a windstorm that was fierce enough to make me question the wisdom of choosing our campsite. Isolated on a sandy peninsula, the water around us deformed into demonic ripples with whitecaps and spray that blew across the surface at speeds I had never witnessed. Amidst this churning phenomenon, I felt small and extremely vulnerable.

When such feelings dominate, positive creativity is out of the question. I became a reactor, projecting all sorts of worst-case scenarios. *What if we can't sail out of this canyon? What if the water rises? What if we run out of supplies?* My faith, logic, rationality and creativity were momentarily blown away by the wind and stinging sand. I began planning an exit strategy, willing to abort this trip that we had planned for so long.

Sometime in the night, however, still under that sandblasted blanket of chaos, something in me solidified. I found my point of strength that brought me to my spiritual senses. In the morning I announced to Beth that I was prepared to stay. As if to challenge that decision, the wind came up again. I grabbed my video camera and began filming it. I told Beth that I thought we should get on our boats, a pair of sailing kayaks with outriggers, and get out in it. With sails down, that was what we did. Though we were blasted again and again, I discovered that I had no fear. I knew we could sail out when the time came to leave.

What a blessing it was to stay! I shudder to think of the experience we would have missed had I given in to my fear. How much we must miss because we listen to our fears rather than stay the course we set for ourselves.

Everyone of us can find justification for the fears that tempt us to turn back because the path we are on is suddenly threatening. What would happen if we pushed on, waited out the storm, taken its best shot and actually embraced the challenge it threw at us?

It occurred to me that the wind was not evil. It was one of the very forces that sculpted the beauty in which we were immersed. It had shaped everything around us, and now it had helped shape me into something better and stronger! It had helped me discover that it was possible to find strength and creativity in the face of fear.

A Message from Clutter

Not all of life is dramatic and adventuresome. Most of it, in fact, is not. Last week, Beth and I were sailing Lake Powell. This week I was faced with the daunting task of cleaning out a section of my garage. I was confronted with a scrap pile of boards too short to be of much immediate use but too long to throw away. I would almost rather be dealing with a cyclone on Powell than attempting to bring order to that pile. It seems that whether one is locked in a mortal struggle with the weather or bringing order to some cluttered pocket around the house, there are spiritual lessons to be learned.

What spiritually significant lesson could possibly come from cleaning out a pile of scrap wood? This type of clutter represents the habit of saying, "I'll put you here now and deal with you later." Do this enough times and you have one big accumulation of unresolved issues. Granted, each issue, like a short stick of lumber, is small. Put them together in a stack, however, and you suddenly have an energy-draining pocket of consciousness.

Does this have an impact on your quality of life? Prosperity gurus like Catherine Ponder certainly thought so. She recommended cleaning out our closets, ridding ourselves of unused clothing and artifacts as a means of kick-starting the flow of creative energy. It works. As I ploughed into that pile, I discovered that I could stop saying to myself, "One of these days I'm going to straighten that stack of wood." Such a thought is actually a weight to our consciousness, a pocket of stored energy that could be directed in a more creative and beneficial way. It's like an accumulation of debris in a river that causes silt and the scum of stagnation to accumulate.

Clearing out such pockets is indeed an adventure in self-discovery. You find that when you let go of clutter, a freer aspect of yourself emerges, a part of you that has always been there but was bound by this seemingly insignificant weight of neglect.

Try tackling one or two of these this week, paying special attention to the lightness that comes with your action. Clutter is simply a signal that it's time to let go and move on.

Doing and Being

> Doing is secondary to being. When we are consciously the Truth, it will radiate from us and accomplish the works without our ever running to and fro.
>
> – Emilie Cady

Despite the advice given in the letter of James, to be doers of the word rather than hearers only, it is of utmost importance to first experience some measure of the truth we seek. We should strive to *be* rather than to always *do*. We do many things to try to incorporate spiritual principles into our thinking. We read, we listen to instructional messages and we engage in service to others. It's important to first be still and know and to get some sense of the inner light, that pure, renewing life energy that radiates from the center of our being.

I have had people ask, "What does your church do for our community?" By virtue of our existence, we offer a service that is rare among churches. Being who we are as a church is, in fact, the greatest service. We fill a spiritual void that goes unaddressed by those who engage in focusing on the material needs of the world.

This is not to imply that such endeavors are unimportant. But this ministry was born because traditional churches are so busy proselytizing and carrying out their missionary works around the world, they neglect the spiritual awakening of the people they serve. Our primary focus has always been on the individual and the importance of tuning in to the still small voice of God within. Whether or not the world knows it, this is the thing they value beyond all theology and the doing of good works.

When you consider your own path, how much of your energy is devoted to letting go and seeking an awakening to the inner presence? Perhaps you have a daily devotion. Do you spend this time reading and discussing with others ideas that are important to you? Or, do you lay everything down, go alone, and seek a deeper experience with the inner light of God's warm presence? Cady suggests that by going within, the light will radiate from us and accomplish the works without our ever running to and fro. By doing only, we lose sight of the light. By letting the light shine from within, we find our center and accomplish the works as well.

Trying to Love

If you are trying to love others and trying to be more loving in general, you are thinking of love from a limited perspective. Don't try so hard to love, but rather focus on opening yourself to the presence of love and affirm that you are the channel through which greater love is now expressing.

Give Yourself to Love

> Love dissolves everything unlike itself.
>
> – Charles Fillmore

Love has been called, *the great attractor*, and for good reason. We are all drawn to loving acts and words of our friends and families, and to the unconditional acceptance of our pets. Love nurtures us, assures us, comforts us in our strongest moments and in our times of uncertainty. This is, no doubt, why John concluded that *God is love*, the most desirable, all-encompassing quality that we can experience.

Yet, as Fillmore points out, love is not only a great attractor, it is also a great dissolver. Love dissolves everything unlike itself. This means that love not only draws greater good, it dissolves conditions that keep greater good from flowing into our lives. Sometimes we are not aware of the conditions that need dissolving, and so we cling to them as if their dissolution is a threat to our very existence. This has led some to believe that love is a double-edged sword that can heal or wound. When love is left to do its perfect work, however, the results are always in our favor.

When you say, "I give myself to love," you are expressing a willingness to let love enhance your strengths and dissolve your weaknesses. Are you prepared to allow love to dissolve a weakness, even when you consider it a strength? Some of the qualities we consider strengths are little more than stones that make up the wall protecting a fragile self-image. Love, like a dentist who knows how to spot a problem tooth, knows exactly what needs to go.

Affirm, *Divine Love is doing its perfect work in me now.* Feel God as a loving presence. Open your mind and heart to dimensions of growth in every area of your being, conscious and unconscious. See love pouring into every aspect of your life, to balance, heal, harmonize and dissolve those things that stand in the way of your greater good.

Love is working in your behalf, so give yourself to love in absolute trust that those things which fall away need to do so, and those things that come to you are there by divine appointment.

The White Stone

> I will give him a white stone with a new name written on the stone which no one knows except him who receives it.
>
> – Revelation 2:17

Every holiday is grounded in some spiritual principle. Though we tend to think of it as a secular holiday, the New Year celebration is no exception. With the dawning of a new year, we turn our thoughts to letting go of the past so we can move unencumbered into new, more prosperous levels of experience.

There is an even deeper significance to the idea of new beginnings. From a spiritual point of view, there is only a beginning. The past is irrelevant. Every new moment is alive with all the potential that has ever been or ever will be. What you have done or have failed to do has nothing to do with what you can do now. Spiritually, you are ageless, not a day older than you were yesterday. Everything you hope to glean from your dreams exists in its fullness within you right now.

This all sounds fantastic, but it's true. The white stone of Revelation is you. The new name written on this stone that only you know is your true nature, your soul.

Touching this white stone, experiencing and bringing your spiritual nature to the forefront of your awareness is the goal of all spiritual education. This is not an end to be reached, but a disposition from which to live your life. As you come alive with your spiritual vitality, your world is transformed. You bring your full being into everything you do. There are no longer sacred moments or special events. Every moment becomes sacred and every event shimmers with special light.

In your quiet times, practice seeing yourself as a vibrant center of eternal life, free of all limitation, all weights of past experience, and free of all apprehension of the future. You have already received the white stone with a new name. Open your mind to this transforming truth.

New Beginnings

Life unfolds in cycles. If you observe these cycles, you will see that there are times when things seem to be falling apart and other times when they are falling in place. We're often confronted with this classical question: *Is the cup half-full or is it half-empty?*

This question points to an important idea that we should keep in mind. Your answer is not determined by the condition of the cup, but by how you feel while viewing it. If you are optimistic and full of expectation, the cup will appear to be half full. If you are feeling weak and vulnerable, beat by unruly circumstances, the cup will seem half-empty.

Many spiritual teachers have adopted as a standard principle the notion that *life is consciousness.* The phrase is intended to suggest that the condition of the cup need not determine how you feel. Determine how you feel and the condition of the cup will take care of itself.

Have you noticed during one of your low moments, how easily an encouraging word or phrase from a book or a bible verse can suddenly inspire you to a new way of seeing? A cup that looked half-empty moments before now suddenly becomes half-full ... and filling. *Do not get discouraged in your emotionally low moments*! Refuse to set your course by these brief seasons of low visioning. Always remember that in the "twinkling of an eye" everything can change, because you allow yourself to change the way you see.

Each new moment is a potential new beginning. It does not matter how negative you have been even one moment ago. You can start now to set a new energy in motion. Create a positive, encouraging affirmation and begin saying it, grasping the joy and emotional expectation that lays the groundwork for your success.

Refuse to be the victim of circumstance or personality. In those moments when you slip back into the *half-empty* mode, remember that life is dynamic, that there is every reason to hold to even the tiniest glimmer of hope, declaring that the good you desire, or something better, is now coming forth.

Recognize Your Good

> The kingdom of God is as if a man should scatter seed upon the ground, and should sleep and rise night and day, and the seed should sprout and grow, he knows not how. The earth produces of itself, first the blade, then the ear, then the full grain in the ear.
>
> Mark 4:26-28

Jesus was a master at using simple agricultural metaphors to explain abstract metaphysical processes. On the topic of manifesting the desires of our hearts, he reveals, in the above passage, two very helpful bits of information. First, when you scatter seed, an invisible force takes over and causes that seed to grow. You are responsible for the sowing, not the growing. Second, once the seed starts to grow, it follows an orderly process that begins in such a humble way that you may not recognize something is actually happening.

Holding a mental and emotional vision is the equivalent of sowing seed. This is how we, as individuals, were designed to be supplied. We are given a mind capable of initiating any material condition we desire. We hold to the ideal, sleep and rise night and day, and the ideal begins to manifest, we know not how. We do not need to know how. That is not our department.

When the manifestation begins to occur, we often do not recognize it. It may appear as a feeling of success, or a change in circumstances so slight that we consider it inconsequential. Plant a field of wheat and it will first appear as grass. Because you know what you planted, however, you know you are seeing the potential for sacks of flour.

Keep your vision on the *full grain in the ear* but learn to recognize and give thanks for the *blade* when it appears. The slightest change in circumstance is evidence that your desire is manifesting. If you pray for abundance and find a dime on the street, think of it as the first blade of manifestation. Soon you will see other blades, and these will grow into the ears, that condition or thing you desire, or something better.

Travelers Through Eternity

You have no doubt had the experience of feeling concern over some appearance, when you open a book and find a line that reminds you of the very thing you need. This happened to me during a challenging moment. I was walking by our bookshelf and Emilie Cady's book, *How I Used Truth*, caught my attention. When I opened it, these lines drew my attention:

> Everything undesirable passes away if we refuse absolutely to give it recognition by word, deed, or thought as a reality. This we can the more easily do when we remember that nothing is real except the eternal.

What a healing balm these words were in that moment of uncertainty! She reminded me that my faith had been in the temporal appearance rather than the changeless, eternal reality that lies behind all things. In an instant, my vision was healed. Today, though I have forgotten that all-consuming issue, I can still recall the words of Cady.

Nothing is real except the eternal. Speak these words quietly to yourself. Speak them as you gaze upon that upsetting issue that currently looms before you. There is a larger realm, a freer expanse of possibility than you are seeing at this moment. Turn your faith to this broader realm and relax in the knowledge that the limiting appearance will pass.

How far has each soul traveled? I doubt that many of us can readily comprehend the scope of our journey that extends well beyond our conscious memory. Knowing specifics about this journey, however, is not nearly as important as reminding ourselves that we are, and will always be travelers through eternity.

Refuse to Quit

> Jesus said to him, 'No one who puts his hand to the plow and looks back is fit for the kingdom of God.
>
> Luke 9:62

A significant number of Jesus' sayings provide straightforward instruction on the practical application of our spiritual resources. Our ability to commit to an ideal is an important example.

We know there is a definite connection between our consciousness and the way our life unfolds. We are beginning to understand that if we can play a role in creating what we see in our experience, we can also play a role in creating what we would like to see. The images we hold of ourselves influence the thoughts, feelings and actions that contribute significantly to our quality of circumstances.

When you use your imagination to form new pictures of changes you would like to see in your life, you discover quickly how easily these new visions are challenged. The old self-image does not just dissolve because you decide you don't want it anymore. You still have plenty of emotion and logic invested. Permanent changes of mind require steadfast commitment. One moment you are determined to hold some wonderful ideal only to find it washed away like a sand castle in an unexpected wave of negative emotion.

Right here is where you will benefit most by calling to mind the advice of Jesus. Regardless of what appearances are saying, despite how you are feeling, put your hand to the plow and keep it there. One moment may indeed bring the appearance of failure, but the next will present the opportunity for success. If you throw up your hands and walk away from your plow, you will not see your opportunity for success. You'll never get your *field* in shape to produce the abundance you desire.

Refuse to quit and you will see your life transform for the better.

God, the Creative Life Force

> God is Spirit, or the creative energy that is the cause of all visible things. God as Spirit is the invisible life and intelligence underlying all physical things. There could be no body, or visible part, to anything unless there was first Spirit as creative cause.
>
> – Emilie Cady

Understanding the nature of God is the first step to understanding how to relate to God. It's probably safe to say that most of us carry a view of God as a human-like, all-powerful figure capable of expressing the full range of human emotion. This is one reason I like to think of God as the creative life force that is active in my being and throughout every aspect of creation. The will of this unseen but all-pervasive force is to express more life, love, power and intelligence through me and through all that concerns me. I do not have to convince God that I am worthy or deserving of the blessings that come with this understanding. My work is to open myself to the greater good that is seeking expression through me now.

In your moments of quiet, you may find it helpful to envision God as the creative life force pressing in upon and expressing through you. Feel yourself stepping out of the way and letting this divine energy move through you in freeing, healing ways. God is personal in the sense that even a small cut on your finger will be healed without your asking. God is universal in the sense that you can trust that your life is divinely ordered, that all the attributes of God are available every moment of every day. In God you live and move and have your being.

God is the source of your being. Work with this idea by affirming something like this:

> *God is my unlimited Source. There is no lack in God. Therefore, there can be no lack in my life.*

This type of statement brings into focus the truth that transcends all self-inflicted, limiting definitions you may have developed.

Spiritual Enlightenment Revisited

One of the unintended, negative consequences of our adopting the idea of soul evolution is that it places the condition of spiritual enlightenment at the end of a series of incarnations. It is, after all, in the very midst of our material experience that enlightenment is needed most. Though we have the Hindu and Buddhist to thank for this model, they are not to blame for spiritually dissatisfied individuals who have merely exchanged their hope for a future heaven to one that anticipates reaching nirvana. Spiritual enlightenment should not be thought of as an end that we would one day achieve. Spiritual enlightenment is a starting place that begins here and now.

The man who found the treasure in the field left it to go sell his other possessions. He was motivated to buy that field and own the treasure (Matthew 13:44). He placed a higher value on the treasure than on the sum of his current possessions. He did this because he was enlightened enough to recognize the value of his discovery. By contrast, the prodigal son left his home, the equivalent of the hidden treasure (to which he ultimately returned), because he did not recognize its value. He believed enlightenment was out somewhere in the far country.

Both men left something of great value, but for entirely different reasons. The first recognized the value of the treasure and devoted all his actions to acquiring it. The second did not recognize the value of what he already had and, like so many who are locked in the evolving soul model, exposed himself to a great deal of unnecessary suffering seeking something he already had. One was spiritually enlightened and the other was not.

Whether or not you are actually in possession of the field is not the standard of spiritual enlightenment. The standard is whether you even recognize the treasure and are willing to let go of the possessions that keep you from buying that field. One of the primary possessions that you must be willing to sell is the belief that your soul is immature, incomplete and that one day you will be enlightened enough to embrace your completeness.

That time is now. If you have captured even a glimpse of this hidden treasure, your value system has been irreversibly changed. Acknowledge that you are now in the process of questioning and letting go of everything that keeps you from purchasing this field, that you are indeed enlightened enough to embrace as a reality your soul's completeness.

The Emerging Soul

> Truly, truly, I say to you, unless a grain of wheat falls into the earth and dies, it remains alone; but if it dies, it bears much fruit.
>
> John 12:24

Considering the context in which this saying of Jesus is presented, we tend to associate it more with his death than with his birth. Yet birth and death, when considered in a spiritual context, are inseparable. You cannot have one without the other.

The birth of Jesus as Savior is symbolic of the birth of the Christ in each of us, that spiritual dimension that Paul referred to as our "hope of glory" (Colossians 1:27). While we've all witnessed the transformation from seed to plant, the mystical birth of Christ involves a renewal of mind (Romans 12:2), a revelation that we are more than our senses-based self-image. The self-image, in fact, is the grain of wheat, the seed to which we must die that the full glory of our soul may come forth.

Paul referred to this process as a mystery that has been hidden for ages, yet mystics of all time have spoken and written of it. People have struggled to understand and experience this elusive light, often with little success.

Jesus gives us the key to this birthing process with the seed illustration. When the grain of wheat is dropped in the ground, it does nothing but let go and surrender to the transformational forces that take over. It is endowed with the intelligence, life, love and power to go through this change. Love softens its outer shell and draws to it the proper nutrients. The death of the grain of wheat is the birth of the new plant that will produce even more grains.

Our spiritual birth, our transformation, is a letting go, a surrendering to a process that transcends the normal intellectual approach to this spiritual awakening. With the same faith we exercise in dropping a seed in the ground, we turn our attention to that inner urge for greater peace and freedom knowing it is our emerging soul that beckons.

The Mythology of Love

> Love never ends; as for prophecies, they will pass away; as for tongues, they will cease; as for knowledge, it will pass away. For our knowledge is imperfect and our prophecy is imperfect; but when the perfect comes, the imperfect will pass away.
>
> 1 Corinthians 13:8-10

These verses from Paul's now famous commentary on the virtues of love express a vitally important idea that has much to teach us. The entire thirteenth chapter (which you may wish to re-read) contrasts the human effort to do good with the enduring nature of love.

Far too often, we see love as a commodity, a possession that we either give or withhold, depending on how safe, bold or generous we feel. We have no reservations about giving love to those who are close to us. They can perform quite obnoxiously and still we love them. That driver who pulled out in front of us, on the other hand, is not as likely to receive the same unconditional treatment, at least not until we discover he did so because he had a medical emergency and was making a desperate dash to the ER. Then we can say, "Okay, I can give you a little more love."

Paul is pointing to the fact that love is not a thing we possess; it is a quality of this eternal, creative life force we call God. When we attempt to be more loving, we are really attempting to stretch our belief that we have only so much love to give and we must be careful how we are going to pass it out. This is more a practice of emotional gymnastics.

If you are trying to love others and trying to be more loving in general, you are likely thinking of love from a limited perspective. Don't try so hard to love but rather focus on opening yourself to the presence of love and affirm that you are the channel through which greater love is now expressing. This way you'll never have to worry about running out of love, and you will let it flow a lot more freely.

The Nearness of God

I'm writing this message from the beach of Coronado, near San Diego. Beth and I are sitting at a table surrounded by overly friendly pigeons, listening to the surf and feeling the cool dampness of the sea breeze.

The sea is often used as a metaphor for God. Its endless horizon, its power, beauty, life and rhythm inspire thoughts and feelings that transcend the norm. Walking down the beach, the rolling waves reach out and touch us, as if to remind us that from any place we stand, we could launch into the deep.

This is true of God as well. Wherever you are, you stand on the shore of the Infinite. Like waves washing the beach, God's presence constantly washes over and through your life in ways that may go unnoticed until you pause to feel the sustaining energy and power that moves in and through you always. You stand at the same door the mystics of all time have stood. You own this door and you are entitled to push it open and enter. The Infinite is your birthright, yours by nature and by the very fact of your existence. Whether you walk in the shallows or swim in the depths, God, your source, sustains you and unveils all the mysteries for you to know.

We humans have created a layer of consciousness that generally does not include attentive interaction with our Source. We are busy running here and there, getting this thing or that, honing one skill or another, immersing ourselves in entertainment, business and events of every kind. It is as if we are walking the beach focused on what the sea may have washed in through the night. It's good to look up at the vast horizon, to contemplate the giver of the gifts sprinkled across the beach. We need no reason to do so. The mind-expanding experience is reason enough.

Look up often. Let the Infinite into your stream of thought. Open your mind to the serene beauty of an inner scene too vast to encompass in thought. Touch that which lifts you beyond ordinary thinking to the level of inspiration that generates new thinking, new emotions and new ideas of who you are and of what your life can be.

From the Inside Out

Man [the individual] is a threefold being, made up of Spirit, soul, and body. Spirit, our innermost, real being, the absolute part of us, the I of us, has never changed, though our thoughts and our circumstances may have changed hundreds of times. This part of us is a standing forth of God into visibility. It is the Father in us. At this central part of his being every person can say, "I and the Father are one" (Jn. 10:30), and speak absolute Truth.

– Emilie Cady

Spirit, soul, and body were three traditionally used terms that Cady employed to model the individual. Some may have difficulty arriving at the intended meaning of these terms simply because our culture makes no distinction between *spirit* and *soul*. The soul, after all, is considered our spiritual nature. I believe it is more clarifying to model the individual as *soul, consciousness* and *body*.

The process we refer to as spiritual growth is an activity that takes place within the consciousness. Changes of consciousness are reflected through the body and our larger body of circumstances. As Cady points out, the spirit, the soul, is the "real being, the absolute part of us, the I of us, [that] has never changed, though our thoughts and circumstances may have changed hundreds of times." Our consciousness is a kind of lens through which we view everything. If we hold onto ideas that are out of integrity with the nature of the soul, we hinder the fuller expression of its true essence. Spiritual growth is the process of bringing our consciousness, the sum of our beliefs, into alignment with what is true of our soul.

As an example, when practicing the affirmation, *"I am now complete,"* you are not referring to your consciousness. This is a reference to your soul. The purpose of the affirmation is to bring your consciousness into alignment with the truth of your soul.

This holds true when you affirm prosperity, divine order, health, peace and any good thing. You are simply stating what is true at your spiritual or soul level and you are opening your mind and heart to let this truth shine forth from the inside out.

The Forgiveness Principle

Forgiveness is the act of letting go of the self that is wounded.

- J Douglas Bottorff

The disciple Peter raised the question of forgiveness. When one offends you, he said in essence, do we forgive them seven times? Jesus responded that you should forgive them "seventy times seven." In other words, forgive until you know you have completely released the offender.

We all have memories of people we feel have hurt us. Why should we let them off the hook when we still carry the scars they inflicted? The answer is simple. A strong identification with that part that feels unjustly wounded will forever keep us in bondage to the actions of others and to certain conditions that threaten to reopen the old wound.

Who would profit more, the person who successfully builds an impenetrable wall of protection around his or her fragile identity, or the one who releases that identity in favor of one that is strong enough to need no protection? A well-built wall, still subject to cracking, is not the equivalent of being firmly grounded in the indestructible soul.

To forgive does not mean that you condone or continue to make yourself the willing recipient of the unacceptable behavior of another. Opening your mind and heart to your spiritual identity changes the relationship dynamic. You make new choices that may include a parting of ways with the offender. This would not occur out of weakness or from a need for self-protection. Your decision is made of the basis of new strength you have discovered.

We become subject to the low vision of others because we carry a low vision of ourselves. Through the practice of forgiveness – self-forgiveness in particular – our vision is raised. We see clearly that our most effective course of action is the inner work of letting go of the self that is subject to wounding. Freedom emerges to the degree that we accomplish this important work.

Understanding Oneness

> Whither shall I go from thy Spirit? Or whither shall I flee from thy presence? If I ascend to heaven, thou art there! If I make my bed in Sheol, thou art there! If I take the wings of the morning and dwell in the uttermost parts of the sea, even there thy hand shall lead me, and thy right hand shall hold me.
>
> Psalms 139:7-10

The idea of oneness among the people of the world has become a primary focus for many of our New Thought friends. I have always believed, however, that the greatest catalyst for positive change is the individual's awareness of his or her oneness with God. This awareness carries the power to lift us from fear, to know that whatever life asks of us, we have the power to rise to the occasion.

God is your unfailing Source. As you affirm this and seek to experience your oneness with God, you are affirming the right outworking of solutions that are for your highest good and the highest good of all that may come into your field of influence. As the Psalmist implies, wherever you go, physically and in consciousness, God is with you.

The common mistake made by those who advocate global oneness and unity among nations is their outside-in approach. The belief is that if we honor diversity and learn to respect differing worldviews, we will all get along and live in peace.

It has been my observation that those who beat loudest the drum of *honoring diversity* usually do so with a condition attached: *Theirs* is the only definition of what it means to honor diversity. Those who do not embrace their particular worldview are dismissed as artifacts of old-world thinking. The *enlightened* collectives see themselves as leaving behind the small-minded flatlanders unable to make the trek up the evolutionary mountain. The divisions between *them* and *us* remain well defined, the notion of oneness as fragmented as ever.

When Emerson pointed out that *souls are not saved in bundles*, he was acknowledging the importance of each person's discovery of their relationship of oneness with God. Like a pebble dropped in a pool, the waves of our conscious unity with God ripple out in a positive motion from center to circumference.

Joining a march for world peace does not assure the inner peace of unity with God. Seek first the inner kingdom of your oneness with God, and the rest will fall in place.

The Light of Compassion

The more we give our light to the world, the more we realize that we already dwell in the house of the Lord. Being a conscious giver opens our eyes to things we cannot see when we are drawn in upon ourselves. The world becomes a brighter place because we bring the needed light of compassion.

The Power of Perseverance

> In a certain city there was a judge who neither feared God nor regarded man; and there was a widow in that city who kept coming to him and saying, 'Vindicate me against my adversary.'
>
> Luke 18:2-3

In this parable, the widow's persistence pays off. The judge, weary of being pestered by the woman, finally grants her the vindication she desires. The parable is presented as a lesson in why one should "pray always and not lose heart."

The judge's response to the woman's perseverance is notable. "For a while he refused; but afterward he said to himself, 'Though I neither fear God nor regard man, yet because this widow bothers me, I will vindicate her, or she will wear me out by her continual coming.'"

Because many of us grew up thinking of God as the great old man that is too busy running the universe to address our personal needs, we would naturally assume that Jesus was using the judge as a reference to God. We'll get more out of this parable, however, if we see the judge as an element of our own consciousness.

I have suggested that God as the creative life force works through each of us in much the same way this force works through the countless blades of grass in our lawns. When you mow your lawn, you create a healing need for each blade. The creative life force responds uniquely and precisely to every single blade of grass. This force does not say, "Just look at all that grass! And every single blade is demanding something of me!" The omnipresent, omnipotent healing force begins its work the moment each blade is cut.

This same force is at work in you and me. We do not have to overcome God's reluctance. Our work in prayer is to hold fast for the good we seek, to affirm this or something better and to persevere in holding and acting on the inner promptings of guidance that unfold through us.

"Ask, and it will be given you; seek, and you will find; knock, and it will be opened to you. For every one who asks receives, and he who seeks finds, and to him who knocks it will be opened" (Matt. 7:7-8).

The Wellspring of Good

> Hitherto we have believed that we were helped and comforted by others, that we received joy from outside circumstances and surroundings; but it is not so. All joy and strength and good spring up from a fountain within one's own being; and if we only knew this truth we should know that, because God in us is the fountain out of which springs all our good, nothing that anyone does or says, or fails to do or say, can take away our joy and good.
>
> – Emilie Cady

This statement represents an important truth that is easily overlooked. We are never separate from the depth and quality of life we desire. Our good only feels separate because we have turned from the inner and relied on the outer to bring us the satisfaction we seek. Sometimes our circumstances are favorable and sometimes they are in disarray. Our focus on them causes an inner fluctuation that we seek to stabilize by seizing control of things in the outer, a perpetual struggle that we never quite win.

When we read that God in us is the fountain out of which springs all our good, we may agree and start looking to God as little more than our great problem solver.

From this perspective, it isn't likely that we will tap the inner fountain to which Cady refers. Whether we are doing our own problem solving or asking God to do it for us, we are still of the same mindset that erodes the peace and satisfaction we seek. We're employing a different method, but we're still attempting to achieve the same end.

Cady is talking about something more than solving problems. She is talking about developing an awareness of God as the source of our being. Our dependency on things and circumstances for contentment has made us blind to our perpetual source of contentment and placed us on an endless track that has no satisfying end.

Practice the presence of God by spending time letting go of your need to harmonize conditions. The harmony you seek is within you. As you begin to experience it, you will find that it does indeed become the fountain from which springs all of your good.

The Scope of Life

When we think of our life, we normally do so from within the reference of our body-based self-image. Our attitudes and perspectives are formed by the current condition of our body and our larger body of circumstances. This causes us to see things in one way when there is another.

You've probably had the experience of flying. One moment you're on the ground making your way through a long, spacious corridor, carry-on in tow, the sights and sounds of the bustling airport occupying your attention. Shortly after, you're seated nearly five miles above the earth, so high that another airport slowly passing below becomes distinguishable only by its huge runways.

On those occasions when we become lost in the details of our daily life, there is something about stepping back and getting a broader view that helps remind us of the larger scope. We are much more than this personality at the center of our swirl of circumstance.

I believe that our present life is but one of many we've experienced. I think of the various places I've lived just within this lifetime. Each involved many relationships, circumstances, dreams and plans that seemed important at the time. These are individualized segments of life into which I was born and to which, in a very real sense, I died. They all had beginnings and they all had endings, whole lifetimes complete in themselves, as different from one another as beads on a necklace. The common thread that runs through them all is me. While each experience has had its own impact, the *I* that I am, the one observing this string of beads, remains the same observer still. My body has aged and I have more beads on my string, but I am still the same. Taking a seat high above this present lifetime, how many other lifetimes might I have strung on the macro-cosmic necklace that constitutes my soul's experience?

While I do not have a conscious recollection of other beads, I do have the absolute conviction that my present life is but one of many. From this perspective, those occasional attention-absorbing problems become nearly imperceptible curiosities passing slowly below.

The Tie that Binds

> I will give you the keys of the kingdom of heaven, and whatever you bind on earth shall be bound in heaven, and whatever you loose on earth shall be loosed in heaven.
>
> Matthew 16:19

One of the most important features found in the teachings of Jesus is his understanding of the relationship between God and the individual. This understanding is important, not for its futuristic impact, but for its impact on daily life. "God is Spirit," he said, "and those who worship Him must worship Him in spirit and in truth." God is invisible, like a breath of air, but very real and very responsive. This presence permeates all, but most importantly, it permeates and is responsive to each person.

God does not respond to us on a capricious whim, but by law. In the above statement, Jesus points out why our life unfolds the way it does. If you think of "earth" as your mind and "heaven" as the creative process of God, you see that Jesus was talking about the process of converting spiritual energy into the material layout of our life-scape. To bind something on earth is to form a definite mental and emotional image of it and then charge this image with enough faith to bring it about. The unseen, formless energy of Spirit then goes to work to bring into manifestation that which you have *bound* in your own consciousness. Thus, what you bind on earth, or latch onto in your mind, assure that the universal, creative process of Spirit will follow suit.

To begin to create a new life through this binding process, you must first embrace your life just as it is. If you are thinking of your life as a kind of prison from which you must escape, you are creating barred doors that will prevent your freedom. Accept that you have brought about the life you are experiencing and begin blessing the good that abounds. Hold a vision of your life as healthy and getting healthier. In creating a vision of where you would like to go, include much praise and thanksgiving for where you are.

This is an important key to a more abundant and prosperous life.

Consciousness

> The earth was without form and void, and darkness was upon the face of the deep; and the Spirit of God was moving over the face of the waters. And God said, 'Let there be light'; and there was light.
>
> Genesis 1:2-3

When we read these familiar lines, our minds most likely shoot back to primordial times of our cosmic beginnings. We envision a state where things are just kind of there, a formless nothingness that is void of life, emotion and lacking any kind of meaningful and progressive activity.

For some, this chaotic state may be a more apt description of their current life. Things are just kind of there, a formless nothing that holds little of interest. It all seems to be just a meaningless panorama floating by.

If you have such a life, these verses hold an important key for change. Notice that nothing of the dark void changes until God speaks in a specific manner. By specific, I mean that God is neither describing nor complaining about the condition of the situation. God is not saying, "Would you just look at this mess! Nothing makes any sense. What am I supposed to do about this?" No. In spite of the conditions, God makes an affirmative statement, "*Let there be light.*" And there was light.

It is doubtful that this ancient Hebrew writer held an accurate view of the literal beginnings of this universe. It is certain, however, that he had a clear view of the transformative principle of the spoken word.

Most of us are experts at describing negative conditions. We may even feel obligated to do so. After all, it is what it is, we say. Why fool ourselves? Fortunately, one new idea, one new insight can change the way we see everything. One moment chaos can reign in your mind, the next moment that chaos can become a field of infinite possibilities just waiting for you to sit up and take charge.

When spoken with the understanding that the full power of God is behind you, these simple words, *let there be light*, can provide a major catalyst for new opportunities and positive change. Instead of describing things as they appear, affirm, *let there be light*, and there will be light.

The Paradigm of Oneness

God as life, love, power and intelligence is the underlying reality of the universe.

Each soul is complete, an individualized expression of the life, love, power and intelligence of God.

The relationship between God and the individual is eternal oneness.

The Paradigm of Oneness

The key to understanding the logic behind any religion is found in understanding that religion's view of the nature of God, the nature of the individual and the nature of the relationship between God and the individual. Those who view God as something separate from the individual operate from a paradigm of separation. Those who view God and the individual as one, operate from a paradigm of oneness.

True metaphysical thinking is based on the paradigm of oneness. Rather than thinking of God as a human-like figure who resides in the sky, we recognize God as omnipresent life, love, power, and intelligence individualized in and as each one of us. The presence of God does not ebb and flow, does not give and withhold or act in love today and fume in anger or vengeance tomorrow.

People often wonder why God seems to ignore human suffering. This question arises when we attempt to give God human characteristics. One moment it seems that God is offering a helping hand, the next moment He is turning His back on those in need.

The understanding of God as omnipresence means God is changeless and completely accessible to all people at all times. "Every good endowment and every perfect gift is from above, coming down from the Father of lights with whom there is no variation or shadow due to change" (James 1:17).

Think of a bright, sun-filled day. One person is out enjoying the sun while another hides away in a dark and musty cellar. We would not accuse the sun of giving its enlivening rays to one and withholding them from the other. We understand that the relationship a person has with the same sun is determined by the choices each are making. God is equally present to all people. One who believes they have offended or angered God places him or herself in a dark cellar of belief. In that "cellar" of negative thought, they can beg and beseech God to forgive them, but they are only being punished by their own actions and false belief.

Wherever you are and whatever you are doing, the fullness of God is present. If you need guidance, affirm that the guiding intelligence of God is now opening the way for you. If you need healing, affirm the healing life of God is now manifesting in your mind and body. If you feel a lack of love, affirm that the presence of God as love is now pouring through every aspect of your life. If you feel powerless in the face of overwhelming conditions, affirm the infinite power of God is working through you now to establish conditions of abundance and greater good of all kinds.

You are now one with God. Expand your awareness of this oneness by affirming that God, your present help and infinite resource, is radiating through you right now, in everything that concerns you.

Who Am I?

As we have seen, the paradigm of oneness presents a model that is based on the omnipresence of God, the spiritual nature of the individual and a relationship of oneness between God and the individual. Last week we focused on the nature of God. This week we'll explore our place in this trinity of ideas.

Every person is an expression of God, which means that, at our spiritual core, we are whole and complete. We think of this spiritual core as the soul, God expressing as the individual.

Obviously we are not all manifesting wholeness or a level of satisfaction one might expect from an expression of God. This is because we carry a self-image that is something less than we are at the spiritual level. This self-image resides in our belief system – our consciousness – and it represents a composite of externally oriented ideas that we have embraced as true. Attempting to live a full and happy life from this limited self-image leaves us always looking for ways to compensate for the lack we feel.

Because we are expressions of God, we instinctively know that God can help lead us to the fulfilling life we crave. Our outer orientated thinking has us, at first, looking out to God as if God were an almighty person able to give us the things for which we ask. In time we begin to realize that our feeling of incompleteness is a manifestation of our own false self-perception. Like the prodigal son wandering in the far country, we turn homeward to that inner fountain that is the very source of our being.

This act of turning, of re-learning who we are, is the first step to true prosperity at all levels. As the father clothed his wayward son with the symbols of wealth, so our external life also begins to reflect the spiritual abundance we discover at our core.

Fulfillment comes from the inside out. As you open your mind to your unwavering spiritual source, your outer life begins to reflect the inner treasures that you have been given.

Oneness, What it Means

Attempting to describe our relationship with God as one of unity is difficult because we are trying to understand two defined entities – the individual and God – as being one. We obviously have a consciousness that allows us to say, *I am me, and you are you.* We are two separate individuals. To speak of a relationship between two people must assume duality. Thinking of our relationship with God, however, is different. The challenge we have with this problem stems from our thinking of God as the old man in the sky. We are essentially thinking of God as we would think of another person.

We can see that two light bulbs are two distinct entities. But what of the electricity that generates the light that shines through them? There is no place where the electricity leaves off and the light shining from the bulb begins. The bulb converts electricity into light, but without electricity, the bulb can do nothing. This illustration sheds a different light on Jesus' saying, "Truly, truly, I say to you, the Son [light/light bulb] can do nothing of his own accord, but only what he sees the Father [electricity] doing; for whatever he does, that the Son does likewise" (John 5:19).

God is the power behind our being. Just as all the qualities of electricity are imparted to the light bulb, so the life, love, power and intelligence of God are imparted to each of us. The light bulb would not say, "I alone express all of the world's electricity." Nor would we, as individuals, say, "I alone express all of God." The light bulb, however, could say, "The electricity I express as light is one and the same electricity found the world over." Likewise, the life, love, power and intelligence that express as our soul are the exact characteristics of God. Our relationship with God, therefore, is oneness.

Words are often limiting, and our use of words to attempt to define the unseen can be confusing. The light bulb has a direct experience with the electricity that it converts into light. To truly know our oneness with God, we must open our minds and hearts to the inner, direct experience of God. The most a teaching can do is direct us to the switch that will turn on the light. It is up to each one of us to flip on that switch.

Soul Evolution: Fact or Fiction?

"I sense that we choose to incarnate into a physical body in order to express love, passion, and the full range of other human emotions not available to us separately in the state of pure awareness and Oneness. What if this life on this planet is the main show, where the action is, and where we wanted to be? This reality is a playground of expression. It looks as though we aren't here to learn or gather experiences for the afterlife. There doesn't seem to be much purpose in that because we don't need any of it there. Rather, we're here to experience and evolve this physical universe and our own lives within it. I made my decision to return when I realized that life here was the most desirable state for me at this time. We don't have to wait until we die to experience nirvana. Our true magnificence exists right now!"

Anita Moorjani,
Dying to Be Me

The paradigm of oneness is a set of three principles that provide a starting point, not a conclusion, for our thinking. How we think of the nature of God, the nature of ourselves, and the nature of our relationship with God will guide our thinking as it pertains to our earthly experience.

I present Anita Moorjani's thoughts here because they support an alternative to the concept of an evolving soul. One who sees him or herself as incomplete and evolving will take a different approach to life than one who sees their soul as complete and seeing the physical incarnation as "a playground of expression." The principles that make up the paradigm of oneness do not force fixed outcomes, but provide a wide range of possibilities of thought. Think of the principle of aerodynamics, for example. Adhering to these principles does not mean that only one kind of airplane will result as we apply them. The Wright brother's kite-like apparatus was born from the same principles used to develop the F-18 fighter jet.

I have come to believe that one of the most important shifts in our thinking is the move from *I am incomplete and evolving* to *I am complete and I am here to express my completeness in a way that only I can*. If God is present, then I am an expression of God and I am one with God right now. The doors of deeper meaning must begin to open if I accept this truth and approach every situation as if it is an important aspect of the "main show."

The Healing Principle

As a spiritual being, I am complete right now. My wholeness radiates through my mind, my body, and my affairs.

The paradigm of oneness, by default, implies a bias toward healing. The soul, being engaged in a perpetual interaction with God, its limitless source, is the very life, love, power and intelligence that constitute the cornerstone of health.

Because much of our identity is rooted in our physicality, we tend to associate our state of health with the current condition of the body rather than with the eternal condition of our soul. From this body-oriented perspective, we can only be as healthy as our aches and pains allow. Seeing our physical nature as the soul's interfacing vehicle, on the other hand, casts a very different light on our approach to healing.

In your quiet times, a helpful visualization is to think of your soul as a brilliant, radiating center of light that is now shedding its healing rays out through your body. Think of any ailment as a shadow naturally and easily erased by the light that you are. Do not think of healing as a thing you have to do. Think of it as a natural act of letting go and letting your light of wholeness shine. See your body engulfed in the rich light of your soul.

The same principle holds true with your larger body of circumstances. Think of yourself as a center of dynamic energy, your wholeness rippling without effort through your body and circumstances in concentric waves of life, love, power and order. Use this affirmation often throughout your day:

As a spiritual being, I am complete right now. My wholeness radiates through my mind, my body and my affairs.

Practice this shift of perception in every circumstance throughout your day until it becomes habitual. You are complete. Let your healing light of completeness shine.

The Consciousness Factor

The paradigm of oneness states that each individual is an expression of God, whole and complete. On the surface, this does not appear to be true. Even the casual observer sees a very wide range of human failures and successes that would seem to indicate otherwise. There is indeed much discrepancy in the way people express themselves. Some have accepted their spiritual wholeness and expect success in all their endeavors. Others affirm that they are incomplete, unworthy, totally separate from anything they consider fulfilling. In both cases, the outer life reflects their attitudes.

An individual can be spiritually whole but be so unaware of his or her wholeness that they live out their entire life from a system of false beliefs. This is the consciousness factor. The beliefs we hold do not change our core nature, but they do influence the way we express ourselves.

At the nucleus of our system of beliefs is a self-image. How you see yourself determines the standard of beliefs you hold. If you see yourself as a worm of the dust, you will entertain beliefs that support this self-image. Likewise, if you truly grasp your spiritual wholeness, your beliefs will reflect this truth.

The problem most of us encounter is that we try to change our belief system without shifting to a more accurate spiritual self-image. It's possible to change what we profess to believe but still maintain a faulty self-image. Ultimately, it is the self-image rather than our professed beliefs that is reflected through our life. Jesus spoke of the good man drawing from his treasure of good, while the evil man draws from this treasure of evil. This saying becomes clear when we think of the "treasure" as the self-image to which we cling.

Understanding the consciousness factor sheds needed light on conditions that, at first glance, might be construed as divine favoritism. It's also important to understand that the belief system we adopt cannot transcend the way we see ourselves.

The practice of meditation is the process that will move you from the paradigm of separation to a paradigm of oneness. You become willing to let go of everything you believe is true about yourself and affirm that your spiritual center is now shedding its light throughout your life. It is not enough to read or hear about this process. The actual experience of your wholeness, your oneness with God, provides the vital element that transforms your consciousness. As you expose yourself to the true light that you are at your soul level, you find yourself thinking about every aspect of your life with greater confidence and optimism.

End of series.

The Choice is Yours

Let what you say be simply 'yes' or 'no'; anything more than this comes from evil.

Matthew 5:37

This instruction from Jesus may seem like an oversimplified, black-and-white approach to life that might better be described in multiple shades of gray. How practical is this advice?

It becomes very practical when we think from a quality of life point of view. By quality of life, I'm referring to our current state of mind, our thoughts, feelings and attitudes. At this moment, you are saying 'yes' to your current state of mind and 'no' to everything else.

Yes is an affirmative position that we associate with faith. *No* is an activity of denial that we associate with release. In terms of your current state of mind, do your present choices represent the quality of life you want to experience? Are you saying *yes* to a line of thought, feeling and attitude that is not in harmony with the quality of life you want to experience?

Think of this as a sprayer attached to the end of a garden hose. When you squeeze the handle, water comes out – *yes*. When you release the handle, the flow of water stops – *no*. In the heat of summer, you may see areas in your lawn that are not getting the needed water. You say *yes* to these areas by spraying them and *no* to those areas that may be prone to produce unwanted growth.

The important point here is to become conscious, with each moment, of the things to which we are saying *yes* and *no*. When we worry, we are saying *yes* to a quality of life that does not support our desired experience. We shut off the spray and change our aim, turning our energy in a direction that is supportive of the quality of experience we want. In this regard, reading something inspiring may help redirect our thoughts, emotions and attitudes in creative new directions that before had not occurred to us.

Your life is yours. The choices you make on how to live it are yours as well. Even if you are influenced by others, your hand is the one squeezing or releasing the sprayer handle. It is indeed a simple process, and the secret is to be conscious that the choices you make are indeed yours.

Praying for Others

The act of praying for others, also known as intercessory prayer, can be a comforting, strengthening and very powerful practice. When you know others are praying with you in your time of need, your faith is strengthened through their prayer support. You do the same for others when you include them in your prayers.

For those of us who see prayer as a way of bringing our consciousness into alignment with what is true of God, of ourselves and of those for whom we pray, we may have questions about our approach. If we're not praying to influence God to produce specific outcomes, why bother to pray at all?

It's important for us to realize that the healing, harmonizing, prospering activity of God is in full swing always. When we pray for another, this is the first thing we should bring to mind. We know the truth that God is working in and through them in beautiful and productive ways. To know this, we release the image we hold of the one for whom we are praying as sick, troubled, financially challenged or whatever appears to be true now. Once we set aside the "facts" of their case, and we visualize them in a healthy, happy and robust condition, mentally ask their forgiveness for seeing them in a lesser state and then see them granting you forgiveness.

This is a very good way to begin, for prayer has been described by some as worry with our eyes closed. We want to abolish worry and fear and hold the truth that God is fully active in all people right now. When we truly come to know this about the one for whom we pray, we experience a deep sense of peace concerning them. We then release them into the perfect outworking of divine love and wisdom. From this point on, every time we think of this person throughout our day, we return to our place of peace. If fear and concern begin to creep in, we again set aside a special time when we ask their forgiveness, re-establish our peace about them and then go about our business knowing the truth that God is present and active in their experience.

This is the kind of affirmative prayer that makes you a positive influence for others. Do not concern yourself with *if* or *how* it works. Just know that God is always at work and you are in perfect alignment with this work.

The Attitude of Gratitude

> Rejoice always, pray constantly, give thanks in all circumstances; for this is the will of God...
>
> 1 Thessalonians 5:16-18

In this first letter to the Thessalonians, Paul gives us a very important key to developing a prosperous life: *give thanks in all circumstances*. Notice he does not say, give thanks *for* all circumstances. He states that we give thanks in the midst of everything that transpires.

To give thanks for all circumstances is a subtle way of saying; whatever happens must be the will of God. It's not a great leap to assume that, because your current circumstances may be difficult, God intends for you to suffer. To give thanks *in* all circumstances opens your mind to external changes for the better.

It is understood that giving thanks for something before it appears is one way of bringing that condition into your life. An attitude of gratitude creates an atmosphere conducive to the manifestation of our desired good. If we wait until after the fact to be grateful for the things we desire, then we may never be grateful at all. We will always be grasping for more, seeking in every person and situation ways to get the things we desire. As we open our minds in gratitude and rejoice that greater good is perpetually unfolding through every aspect of our experience, we begin to see the blessings mount. An attitude of gratitude takes your mind off yourself and your problems and moves you from being self-centered to Self-centered, a shift that gives you a much wider context of possibilities.

Regardless of your current circumstances, develop an attitude of gratitude. Count your blessings and give thanks for the good things that are unfolding through you now. Though you cannot see the immediate benefit of doing so, stimulate your thinking and the flow of creative ideas by giving thanks for opportunities to do new things that inspire you to see your life differently. An open and grateful mind and heart is a powerful catalyst for positive change.

In all things, starting with your life as it is, begin giving thanks. Then watch as your life immediately takes a turn for the better.

The Call from Home

> Hitherto we have turned our heart and efforts toward the external for fulfillment of our desires and for satisfaction, and we have been grievously disappointed. The hunger of everyone for satisfaction is only the cry of the homesick child for its Father-Mother God. It is only the Spirit's desire in us to come forth into our consciousness as more and more perfection, until we shall have become fully conscious of our oneness with All-perfection. Man never has been and never can be satisfied with anything less.
>
> – Emilie Cady

For me, one of the outstanding features of Emilie Cady's teachings is her ability to instill the feeling of familiarity. Though I was quite young when I discovered her work, something in me felt like I had come home, as if some lost connection I had forgotten had been restored.

By social and cultural default, we have been trained to seek outside of ourselves the remedy for that nagging feeling that something deep and important is missing. In truth, nothing is missing. We have simply been programmed to look in all the wrong places for the satisfaction we intuitively crave. Like the prodigal son, we have pursued this missing element in the far country of accomplishments, positions, money, relationships and a host of other things that promise but fail to satisfy our spiritual homesickness.

When we read or hear words from our spiritual home, we know they are true. Everything in our being recognizes them. We need no one to confirm they are true. The prodigal son was not advised to go home. On his own he reached the point of knowing he was away from his real home. Severe lack forced him to *come to himself*, arise and go to his father. Heeding this call, his homesickness was cured and he was clothed in abundance.

The power of this parable is found in the fact that it is about you and me. We are each receiving this call from home. Let us come to ourselves, rise and return to our spiritual home.

The Prayer Principle

> Therefore I tell you, whatever you ask in prayer, believe that you have received it, and it will be yours.
>
> Mark 11:24

I have written of the power of choice and the need to direct attention to present states of mind to which we are either saying *yes* or *no*. This simple action determines the quality of our inner life. The above instruction on prayer, given by Jesus, is an equally simple idea that again involves mindfulness and choice making. In this case, we define the thing for which we ask and we hold the affirmative state of mind of having already received it.

It's worth mentioning that answers to our prayers may not come as the full-blown vision we hold. They may appear as "first the blade, then the ear, then the full grain in the ear" (Mark 4:28). If we envision only the *full grain in the ear*, we may not recognize the *blade* when it appears. In addition, we should remain open to the possibility there is a better solution to our need than the one we envision. We could be looking for a specific change in circumstances when all that is needed is a slight shift in attitude.

Certainly, a helpful change of attitude is the one that affirms the thing you ask for is already present. The *blade* of the answer you seek may very well be found in completing some task you have been putting off or dismissing altogether. This may seem totally unrelated to your prayer request, but completing such tasks often sparks new inspiration and provides a jump-start to your creative energies.

Holding the attitude that you have already received what you ask for in prayer means that *something of this answer is accessible to you right now*. When you state that there is only one Presence and one power, you are affirming the truth that things that may seem unrelated are actually totally related.

Try doing something you've been putting off. Make no announcement as to why you are doing it, and expect nothing in return. Just do it and see where it leads. If another thing to do comes to mind, do that as well.

Let the thing you ask for in prayer represent a desired state of being. When you pray, be open to this, or a better way of achieving your desired state of being. Pay attention to promptings to action, even when they seem unrelated to your desired goal. Think of your action as the blade, the tender sprout that leads to the answer you seek.

Soul, Consciousness and Body

Soul: The life, love, power and intelligence of God expressed as your spiritual essence. Your soul is complete and totally free now.

Consciousness: The ever-evolving sum of beliefs and ideas you hold. These can be based on the truth of the soul, or they can be based on the restricting ideas of the self-image.

Body: Your physical interface that gives you the ability to interact with the material plane.

Going Alone

> Seek light from the Spirit of Truth within you. Go alone. Think alone. Seek light alone, and if it does not come at once, do not be discouraged and run off to someone else to get light; for, as we said before, by so doing you get only the opinion of the intellect, and may be then further away from the Truth you are seeking than ever before; for the mortal mind may make false reports.
>
> – Emilie Cady

In this passage, Cady is elaborating on a way to pray as mentioned by Jesus: "But when you pray, go into your room and shut the door and pray to your Father who is in secret; and your Father who sees in secret will reward you" (Matthew 6:6).

Jesus was commenting on those who make a public display of prayer, who are more concerned about how they look and sound than with what actually happens in their consciousness.

Information can come from many sources, some good and some confusing. God communicates through direct revelation, in the silence of our being. When we pray and we see a favorable change in our circumstances, we say, "See, God answers prayer." If we see the change of conditions as the answer to prayer, then we assume that when conditions do not change our prayer is not answered. This is usually when we go about seeking the input of others.

The mark of spiritual maturity is seeking God for the sake of knowing God. This we can only do in the inner room of our being. As Cady advises, if the light we seek does not come at once, and it probably won't, don't give into the temptation to seek it elsewhere. The light each one of us seeks is the light that is the life of us, the very essence of our being. It would make little sense to think that our spiritual essence would be located in a place other than our own heart and soul.

A good centering statement is the biblical, "Let there be light." Speak these words calmly and expectantly. Understand that as you speak them, the light is working through your consciousness and into your awareness at that very moment. Be patient and be at peace.

I Am the Vine

> Abide in me, and I in you. As the branch cannot bear fruit by itself, unless it abides in the vine, neither can you, unless you abide in me. I am the vine, you are the branches. He who abides in me, and I in him, he it is that bears much fruit, for apart from me you can do nothing.
>
> John 15:4-5

Using this simple metaphor, Jesus beautifully illustrates the relationship each individual has with his or her spiritual source. God, our creator/sustainer, is like the vine from which we grow. To abide in God is to live with the awareness of God as the source of our being.

Because we often draw our identity from external sources – job, family, social level, etc. – we may feel overwhelmed when challenges sweep through our lives. These words from John remind us to pause, and to reconnect to our source. In the seventh verse, Jesus makes this promise: *"If you abide in me, and my words abide in you, ask whatever you will, and it shall be done for you."*

We abide in God through prayer. Prayer is a two-fold process. First, we are to release the negative energy that has been stirred in us by appearances. This is called, *deni-*

al. Let go of your emotional attachments, your fears, your anger, to that which you do not want. Speak words like this: *I now release all emotions of fear and doubt.* Next, move into the second half of the prayer process by affirming, *God is my source, God is my strength. My life is now unfolding in divine order.*

Allow yourself to experience the lightness of letting go, and the infilling of assurance that your life is unfolding perfectly and according to the divine blueprint that is being imparted from within your being.

In the same way the fruit of the vine manifests from within the branch, so a spiritually ordered life will manifest through your inner being and through every facet of your external life. Abide often in the awareness of God as your source, then ask whatever you will, and it shall be done for you.

Releasing Loved Ones

While living on this earth plane, it seems that we inhabit two worlds. In reality, we inhabit but one world expressing as the material and spiritual dimensions, but for practical purposes, we treat this one as two. When we think of a person, for example, we naturally recall the experiences we've had with them on the material plane. If we browse a photo album, we'll see their physical aspect representing different periods in their life, and we will recall shared moments that make up our thoughts and memories of them.

When we consider who this person actually is, especially if they have now passed on, we think of him or her in a much broader, spiritual context. While we miss our physical interaction, we also hold them in the freeing truth that they continue their life in ways that are at least as beautiful and productive as they were in that fraction of their experience we were privileged to witness. We're saddened by our loss, inspired by what they gave us and we find comfort knowing they are free to continue their experience in living in ways we can only imagine.

What do we do with a loved one who, because of a terminal illness or advancing age, now stands with a foot in each of these two worlds? Do we pray for a miracle?

Do we see him or her as whole and free while affirming that they take up their bed and walk? This is certainly the first inclination of most of us. We assume that it is best for those we love to remain in the physical condition by which we have known them. Our prayer for healing is often a prayer of restoration to this condition.

In such cases, our prayers should always include the vision of our loved ones as whole and free. This is the truth about them. What is also true is that they are neither the physical body nor the composite of circumstances that we have associated with them. They are much more than this. While on earth, they may have played the role of our parent, for example, but the spiritual reality is that they and we are the offspring of the Divine. Our physical bodies are mortal, but our true essence is eternal.

In one sense, we are all transitioning out of this material realm. For some, this transition is a very long process. For others, it is shockingly fast and unexpected. In all cases, however, the laying down of the physical body is inevitable. Our prayer for release is one that holds to the truth of the eternal nature of the soul and affirms the best and highest for those for whom we pray.

It is not our place to name the good of another. It is our place to hold them in the light that their highest good is unfolding, that they are complete, eternal expressions of God right now.

Your Divine Core

> One drop of water taken from the ocean is just as perfect ocean water as the whole great body. The constituent elements of water are exactly the same, and they are combined in precisely the same ratio or perfect relation to each other, whether we consider one drop, a pailful, a barrelful, or the entire ocean out of which the lesser quantities are taken; each is complete in itself; they differ only in quantity or degree. Each contains the whole; and yet no one would make the mistake of supposing from this statement that each drop is the entire ocean.
>
> – Emilie Cady

One of the basic assumptions found in all metaphysical literature is that each person is an expression of God. By this, we mean that the core of every person is divine. How each individual expresses this divinity, of course, varies widely. Much of what we see of the human condition indicates the absence of understanding of this core divinity. The many theological systems that hold each individual is sinful to the core certainly offer little or no help in aligning our thinking with the truth of our oneness with God.

Because we live our lives according to what we believe about ourselves, it is important that we come to the truth that we are spiritual beings expressing through a consciousness that is likely littered with misperceptions that clog our thinking. Our work in spiritual growth is more about letting go of these misperceptions than about becoming better people. To be perfect even as our heavenly Father is perfect is to recognize that perfection already exists, that we are to awaken to it rather than create it.

Think of your true essence as a single drop of pure ocean water existing in and as you right now. Imagine this pure drop expanding into a fountain that literally fills you from the inside out. See this flow continue into and through every aspect of your life and you have a good model for understanding what it means to be an expression of God.

Making God Yours

> You shall love the Lord your God with all your heart, and with all your soul, and with all your mind. This is the great and first commandment. And a second is like it, You shall love your neighbor as yourself. On these two commandments depend all the law and the prophets.
>
> — Luke 10:27

The above statement comes from the Gospel of Luke and, according to the story, was given by Jesus to a lawyer who had asked which of the commandments were most important. We may have read or heard this response from Jesus so many times that we don't stop to consider its importance.

To "love the Lord your God" is the most vital aspect of this statement. Most of us are trying to love the God of another. Though we pay homage to God, we may not be able to say that we know God so well that we can love God completely, with all our heart, soul and mind. Likewise, we might be familiar with the call to love our neighbor while failing to grasp the significance of loving our neighbor as ourselves.

In truth, you can only love what you truly know. Jesus is pointing to the fundamental fact of all spiritual development. He is saying, the first and most important thing you can do is to know God – *your* God. Loving your God is the natural result of knowing God. In your times of quiet meditation, you open yourself to God, and the fullness of God's presence. You begin to experience the love and light that God is and you cannot help but respond by giving your whole being to further knowing your Creator-Sustainer. This becomes the single most important desire in your life, for it puts everything else in place.

Many attempt to love their neighbor but forget the "as yourself" aspect. Again, in your quiet time you begin to see and experience your true spiritual nature that is very different from what you have known of yourself. Love begins to flow from you without effort. You become a light of love in the presence of your neighbors because you see yourself, as you are, a true and beautiful light of the Lord your God.

The Quest for Freedom

Oppressed people cannot remain oppressed forever. The yearning for freedom eventually manifests itself ...

> Martin Luther King Jr

Martin Luther King championed the cause of freedom from racial prejudice and a level of social inequality that today many find difficult to comprehend.

While the desire for freedom includes the need to be free of oppressive social conditions, it goes much deeper than this. We and all living things, desire freedom because we are, at the deepest level of our being, already free.

It is this level of freedom Jesus referred to when he said to his fellow Jews, "You will know the truth, and the truth will make you free" (Jn. 8:32). His audience did not grasp his meaning, for they said, "We are descendants of Abraham, and have never been in bondage to anyone. How is it that you say, 'You will be made free?'"

Jesus answered them, "Truly, truly, I say to you, everyone who commits sin is a slave to sin." The "sin" that most of us commit is that of not knowing the truth, of being consciously out of touch with our spiritual essence.

We may, like Jesus' listeners, be relatively free of imposed, binding restrictions. If we are prone to worry and fear, on the other hand, we are imprisoned by these mental and emotional captors. We can achieve freedom from oppressive conditions while remaining in bondage to internal conflict.

To know the truth that sets us free is to touch that inner flow of unrestricted life that is our very essence. This inner freedom can be experienced regardless of external conditions. Yes, we want freedom in our conditions. This freedom without the inner connection, however wonderful, will not satisfy.

Your quest for freedom is a response to a deep level of yourself that is already free. Meditate on this and invite your unrestricted soul to step forward.

Soul Recovery

> What man of you, having a hundred sheep, if he has lost one of them, does not leave the ninety-nine in the wilderness, and go after the one which is lost, until he finds it?
>
> Luke 15:4

This parable of the lost sheep describes perfectly the notion of the complete soul. Most people on the spiritual path see themselves as owning ninety-nine sheep and dreaming of someday acquiring the hundredth. The parable points out that we are already in ownership of the hundred and one has strayed.

In light of our spiritual quest, the missing sheep represents the soul. The ninety-nine represent our normal, daily awareness that, in itself, seems adequate, though we feel like something is missing. Our flock has not quite reached the magic one-hundred mark of fulfillment. We need that one more sheep of spiritual awareness, which we believe we will acquire with more work and study.

Looking for a thing you have lost is different from hoping for a thing you do not have. The first involves acquisition; the second involves recovery. If we are seeking to acquire spiritual fulfillment, we will likely turn to things outside of ourselves. If we are seeking to recover a spiritual awareness that we already have but have forgotten, we will turn within and wait patiently for its revelation.

The parable also points to a very important aspect that people often overlook. We seem to be satisfied having someone tell us that we actually own one-hundred sheep, even though one has strayed. The parable encourages an all-out search for the missing sheep. The ninety-nine will be fine while we spend time turning our attention away from them in search of the one that is lost.

In meditation, we close our eyes to the ninety-nine and turn our attention to the one, that internal fountain that is our soul. Our attention, our receptivity is grounded in the absolute knowing that the spiritual light we seek now radiates from our spiritual center, the complete soul.

The Freedom You Seek

Prayer, when used as a consciousness raising practice, involves the two aspects of denial and affirmation. The denial side is the releasing of all fear and doubt concerning the status of some situation. In releasing the weight of negativity, there is a natural rising of a positive, more creative energy. We experience this freedom as our mental and emotional burden lifts. The affirmative side of prayer focuses on this natural, often subtle rising of power. Removing the block of fear allows for the free-flow of creative inspiration and new ideas. Focusing this energy with our words is the very essence of affirmative prayer.

You can get a sense of this dual dynamic simply by squeezing your hand into a fist. Hold that position for fifteen or twenty seconds then release it. You'll notice the cool flow of blood into the now relaxed muscles of your hand. When your mental and emotional energy is bottled into a "fist" of fear and worry, you have to make a decision to stop sustaining the fist. This decision is what we're calling *denial* or *release*. When you relax your hand, a natural *affirmation* of circulation occurs. Your hand becomes free of the blockage that caused the discomfort.

It's important to note that both making and relaxing the fist are *choices*. The choice to make the fist blocks circulation, and the choice to relax allows the natural free-flow of blood. When we make a *fist* of worry and fear, this is also a choice. No one or no thing forces us to make this choice, and we are under no obligation to continue making it. This is exactly why Jesus taught that we must not judge by appearances. Appearances will tell us that we *must* make a fist of fear. In truth, there is no such requirement. The appearance, whatever it may be, does not have the power to dictate our choice of whether we make a fist or relax our hand. A relaxed hand, we know, is much more useful than a clenched fist. Likewise, our free-flowing mental and emotional energy is much more useful and creative than energy that is clenched or bottled in fear.

Practice separating external appearances from the inner choices you are making. Physical stress is the manifestation of an emotional clenched fist of fear. Release this fear and open your heart in trust. It is the open heart that receives the freedom you seek.

The Everlasting Arms

God ... is the substance (from sub, under, and stare, to stand), or the real thing standing under every visible form of life, love, intelligence, or power. Each rock, tree, animal, every visible thing, is a manifestation of the one Spirit – God – differing only in degree of manifestation; and each of the numberless modes of manifestation or individualities, however insignificant, contains the whole.

– Emilie Cady

As I read this text, I am reminded of a verse from Deuteronomy:

"The eternal God is your dwelling place, and underneath are the everlasting arms" (Deuteronomy 33:27).

Shifting from the notion that God is a human-like figure who resides in the sky to the understanding that God permeates and sustains all life is a big step for many. And yet, as we make this change in our thinking, we come to know God as an imminent help and sustainer in our times of uncertainty. To think of God as our dwelling place and ourselves as being upheld and guided by God's presence opens our mind to this truth. We take a more peaceful, centered approach to our life.

God is your substance, and the substance of all you desire. This is a prospering statement, one that helps open your mind to the truth of God as your unfailing resource. Instead of thinking "there are four months to harvest," the truth that God is your ever-present substance opens your mind to the "fields ready for harvest" right now. The same is true with health. God is your present source of health. The healing energy that God is, works in and through your mind and body now.

The statement, *I live in God, and God lives in me*, aligns your thinking with the truth of your relationship to God. Speak these words when you are alone, quietly when you are with others, while you are out for your walk, driving your car or alone in a meditative setting. Do not reach out to God. Look within yourself. Wherever you are in life, open your mind to God's prospering, healing presence.

Our Spiritual Home

When we read or hear words from our spiritual home, we know they are true. Everything in our being recognizes them. We need no one to confirm they are true.

The Narrow Gate of Meditation

> Enter by the narrow gate; for the gate is wide and the way is easy, that leads to destruction, and those who enter by it are many. For the gate is narrow and the way is hard, that leads to life, and those who find it are few.
>
> Matthew 7:13-14

Though few will remember it, July 17, 2007 was hailed by millions of people as the beginning of a major shift in human consciousness. The woman leading this movement claimed that during a near-death experience, she was visited by extra-terrestrials who had revealed a plan that would solve all of earth's problems and allow the entire human family to live in an environment of equality, peace and prosperity.

Frankly, in my thirty-plus years of ministry, I have lost count of the number of movements making similar claims, all of which have come and gone.

There is a strong belief held by many that if we band together and make enough noise, something transformative will happen to our planet. But it's not the stadium full of people visualizing and chanting world peace that make a significant contribution to the evolution of human consciousness. It's the individual sitting alone in a quiet corner seeking open communion with the source of his or her being. These are the true pioneers of consciousness, the ones who demonstrate the boundless knowing capacity of the human mind.

There is a strong belief that a *broken earth* is the cause that squelches the development of human potential, that if we could just solve all the problems of hunger, poverty and strife, everyone would have the opportunity to be all they can be.

If earthly conditions were the cause of stifled human development, then there would not be a single person who has made a spiritual breakthrough. Though many use them as an excuse for avoiding the challenging path of spiritual introspection, earthly conditions prevent nothing. If anything, they provide the reason and stimulation to turn within and connect with our eternal anchor.

The salvation we seek always has and always will be found within the realm of our spiritual potential. It is the work of a loving Creator that placed fulfillment within reach of every individual creation. Not even a loving Creator, however, can open the eyes of one who insists that their happiness is dependent on having only certain kinds of external conditions.

The simple truth is the spiritual dimension currently exists in its full glory and is accessible to all who would enter through that narrow gate of meditation.

The Prayer Dynamic

Prayer, in some form, is an integral part of every religion. For some, prayer consists of memorized texts believed to influence God in a favorable way. For others, prayer is more an attitude of positive expectation, a feeling that things are working out for the highest good of all concerned. While there are helpful elements in both approaches, when either is practiced without an understanding of our relationship to God, they can easily become meaningless ritual or ineffective blinders.

When you look for a resolution to some problem, you are really seeking an internal experience of peace, harmony and absolute assurance that everything is all right. You want the external condition to change so you can have this inner experience. Effective prayer begins with the understanding that this inner experience is already available. Embrace it first, and the outer condition will follow.

What stands between you and this desirable inner experience? You may be tempted to blame the condition, but the reaction of fear is really an emotional choice. You are looking at this external thing and assuming that it has the power to make you afraid. As convincing as this may seem, you're making a false assumption. In truth, you were not given a spirit of fear. You were given a spirit of courage and wisdom that is temporarily eclipsed by your choice to entertain fear.

The first step in effective prayer is to realize that, despite appearances, you are in no way obligated to cling to fear. Sit quietly and intentionally allow this negative emotion to dissolve. As you do, you will notice the immediate rise of freedom and power. If it doesn't happen instantly, then you may recall that Jesus noted casting out some of these "demons" requires much prayer and fasting. This simply means that you are clinging tightly to certain negative states, bolstered no doubt by a very convincing appearance. Letting these go will take some concerted effort, and you can succeed.

As I've indicated, strength naturally rises as fear dissolves. Embrace this strength as it comes. Let this new sense of power become your basis of thought and emotion, and you will find yourself moving with greater ease through your difficult time. This rise of strength is the answer that will carry you successfully through any appearance.

Victory in Silence

Victory must be won in the silence of your own being first, and then you need take no part in the outer demonstration of relief from conditions. The very walls of Jericho that keep you from your desire must fall before you.

– Emilie Cady

A common theme throughout Cady's writings is that God, not you, will work through you to bring about desired changes. Your work, as she clearly implies, is to "be still and know."

With most of us, this advice probably runs counter to our own work ethic. *If it is to be, it is up to me.* Little, if anything seems to get done sitting around waiting for God to do something.

Cady, however, does not offer such advice. As we saw in the previous lesson, winning victory in the silence of your own being first is a very definite action. Doing so increases your awareness and inspires right vision and effective action. The crumbling of the walls blocking your good may not be as dramatic as those that fell in Jericho, but their falling will represent no less a victory for you.

What we seek in the quiet is a definite knowing that all is well, that despite appearances to the contrary, things are moving toward a more desirable condition. Going to this inner place is like gaining a vantage point on a trail. You see where you are and you see where you need to go. With this assurance, you move forward in confidence.

Regardless of pressing conditions, set aside time to step back and find that inner place where you truly know all is well. God is now working though you and through your circumstances in ways that assure success. Once you reach this place of inner knowing, carry it with you throughout your day. Remind yourself often that God is using you and those around you to establish order and open new doors of opportunity. When appearances contrary to your desired good present themselves, as they surely will, get into the habit of knowing this too shall pass. Remain centered in God as a harmonizing presence. Carry with you the victory you gain in silence in all that you do.

Peace, be Still

> And he awoke and rebuked the wind, and said to the sea, "Peace! Be still!" And the wind ceased, and there was a great calm.
>
> — Mark 4:39

It's probably fair to say that most of us are attempting to change some set of circumstances so we may experience greater peace of mind. This is understandable, for as we look at circumstances that appear to be out of harmony, we take the appearance into our thought and become disturbed. It is only logical that if we smooth out inharmonious circumstances, we will also experience peace of mind.

There is another way to approach this problem of peace of mind. When Jesus spoke to the high winds and unruly sea he was in exactly the same set of circumstances as his disciples. They were literally in the same boat. The disciple's were focused on the possibility of sinking. Jesus kept his peace. The subtle difference in Jesus and his companions was their state of mind. He was not viewing the storm from a fearful self but from his God-centered awareness.

Meister Eckhart expressed this same understanding.

Truly, if you do not begin by getting away from yourself, wherever you run to, you will find obstacles and trouble wherever it may be. People who seek peace in external things – be it in places or ways of life or people or activities or solitude or poverty or degradation – however great such a thing may be or whatever it may be, still it is all nothing and gives no peace.

If you are in the midst of a storm right now, lay aside, for a time, all attempts to change your circumstances, even through an effort involving prayer. Speak these words, not to the outer appearance of the storm, but to your own inner reaction: *Peace, be still.* Speak them until the waves of fear and the winds of anxiety begin to subside. Find your center of peace and strength. As you enter this center of calm you will see the apparent storm is not so fierce as it seems.

The Gift of Uncertainty

"People wish to be settled; only as far as they are unsettled is there any hope for them."

Ralph Waldo Emerson

I've always resonated with these words of Emerson. For me, they stir something that rings true at the soul level. In my public addresses, I speak often of the universal desire for freedom shared by all expressions of life, including us. Freedom from some level of bondage is frequently on our mind, probably because our "wish to be settled" so often leads us into feelings of being trapped in life's conditions. The English political and military leader, Oliver Cromwell (1599 – 1658) went so far as to say, *"A man never rises so high as when he knows not whither he is going."*

In my book, *A Practical Guide to Meditation and Prayer,* I share an interpretation of the Cain and Abel story (Genesis 4), which beautifully addresses this dynamic. Cain, you may recall, was a tiller of the soil, a farmer. Abel, his brother, was a shepherd. The farmer settles into a single plot of land while the shepherd leads a nomadic life. We might think of Cain as that part of us that wishes to be settled, and Abel as that part that requires freedom to move about. The day comes when both brothers bring offerings to the Lord, Cain, his first fruits of the land, Abel, the firstlings of his flock. The Lord rejects Cain's gift but accepts Abel's.

Taking the story literally, this rejection of Cain's offering is confusing. From a spiritual point of view, however, we see that the Lord, the law of life and expansion, favors the shepherd mindset that seeks no boundaries, that is not settled into a view of life surrounded by the fences of preconception. Cain's slaying Abel represents our own attempts to address our desire for freedom by settling into the attainment of some external acquisition (a fenced plot). That this is not possible is depicted in the Lord banishing Cain to the land of Nod, which in Hebrew means, "wandering." Cain himself is uprooted from his life as a "settled" farmer and forced to become a nomad. In other words, we cannot suppress our inherent desire for freedom because freedom is our natural, spiritual state.

If you are going through a season of uncertainty, know that you are in a position to re-evaluate the mental and emotional boundaries you have placed around yourself. Think of your situation as the gift of uncertainty, a soul-searching opportunity to observe patterns of thought and choice making that serve to confine rather than free you to live the life of your preference.

Yes and No

> You have heard that it was said to the men of old, 'You shall not swear falsely, but shall perform to the Lord what you have sworn.' But I say to you, Do not swear at all, either by heaven, for it is the throne of God, or by the earth, for it is his footstool, or by Jerusalem, for it is the city of the great King. And do not swear by your head, for you cannot make one hair white or black. Let what you say be simply 'Yes' or 'No'; anything more than this comes from evil.
>
> Matthew 5:33-37

If I were to reduce this piece of advice to a couple of lines, I would say it like this: Do not bind your future actions by things you have no control over. Stay in the moment and either accept or let go of each issue as it arises in your mind.

For example, you set a goal for yourself and you say, "I swear to God I'm going to achieve this thing." It will only take a little time, a couple of rattles, and one good blow to get you to break that promise and admit that the thing was too high a goal, or that you didn't deserve it, or it wasn't God's will. If, on the other hand, you set your goal, and each moment you examine your thoughts, feelings, and actions in light of whether they add to or take away from your objective, you have a very different situation. Say 'yes' to the things that add to the completion of your goal and 'no' to the things that do not, and you will eventually accomplish your goal.

Say you want to lose weight. You say 'no' to cake and ice cream and 'yes' to celery. You say 'no' to sitting in front of the television for hours and 'yes' to long, vigorous walks. You say 'no' to affirmations of being fat, and 'yes' to affirmations that associate you with your perfect weight. And this is true in everything.

If you are not succeeding in the achievement of your desires, it is because you are saying 'yes' to things that defeat your vision, and 'no' to things that would advance you.

Become conscious of how you employ this very powerful activity, and every step you take will be the right one.

Your Inner Teacher

> Heretofore we have sought knowledge and help from outside sources, not knowing that the source of all knowledge, the very Spirit of truth, is lying latent within each one of us, waiting to be called on to teach us the truth about all things – most marvelous of teachers, and everywhere present, without money or price!
>
> – Emilie Cady

It may seem backward to think that when we have an external need we would be told to turn within for an answer to the problem. It would seem to make more sense to follow old patterns and busy ourselves seeking external solutions.

Life is much more than a perpetual process of finding temporal solutions to temporal problems. We are spiritual beings who have, for reasons we know at the deepest level, stepped into this earthly experience to accomplish some work important to us. We brought with us our connection to our eternal source of guidance and supply, a resource of wisdom and guidance that will always lead us to the right answers when we need them.

Jesus said, "Ask, and it will be given you; seek, and you will find; knock, and it will be opened to you. For every one who asks receives, and he who seeks finds, and to him who knocks it will be opened" (Matthew 7:7-8). This is a straightforward promise from one who understood better than most the spiritual dynamics of divine guidance.

If you find yourself in a place in your life where you do not know what to do, set aside time to go apart from the clamor of the world and turn within. Move into that place of inner stillness and assurance that all is well, that the answers you need are now coming forth to fill your external needs in ways that work for your highest good and the highest good of all concerned. You may wish to use a simple affirmation that Cady herself found helpful in her own time of need: It is done: God is now manifested as my supply.

The Lord's Prayer Series

Open Your Mind

Part 1 of 6

Our Father, who art in heaven, hallowed be thy name ...

In this first line of the Lord's Prayer, we are exposed to three important ideas. We can think of these ideas as a preparatory mindset that opens us to receive.

Our Father suggests a loving relationship with God. Like most of us today, Jesus was raised in a culture that believed God was capable of punishment. He taught that God would not give you a serpent if you asked for a fish, or a stone if you asked for bread. This form of address carries the idea of God as a supportive parent. How different this is from the attitude that we may not deserve or be worthy of the good for which we ask. We are to approach God as if God were a loving parent.

Who art in heaven carries a meaning that is not readily apparent to the one who thinks of heaven as a place in the sky. Jesus compared heaven to yeast in bread dough, and a mustard seed that expands into a tree. Heaven carries the idea of *expansion*. When you pray, open your mind to new possibilities. Let go of your old perceptions. Allow your level of expectation to expand into the realm of infinite possibility.

Hallowed be thy name is an affirmation of God as wholeness. The wholeness you seek, whether it is in the form of health, a solution to a problem or a prosperity challenge, is present right now. Wholeness is the nature of God. In other words, act as if the thing you seek, that which is for your highest good, is already present. You become receptive and expectant of this good.

Become conscious of these three ideas. Practice them all whether or not you use them with this prayer. They will help open your mind to the good you desire.

The Expansive Action of God

Part 2 of 6

Thy kingdom come, thy will be done, on earth as it is in heaven.

Like the first line in the *Lord's Prayer*, this second line also expresses three ideas that are important to a prayerfully receptive state. It is generally believed that this prayer is petitionary, that it is making requests of God. Many modern biblical scholars, however, tell us we should think of this prayer as affirmative in nature, that it should be spoken in a manner similar to this: *Thy kingdom is here; thy will is being done, on earth as it is in heaven.*

This attitude aligns our thinking with the truth that the fullness of God (kingdom of God) is here and the will of God (absolute good) is unfolding right now. In relation to a challenge you may be undergoing, you are to think of God's help as already present and only absolute good is unfolding through your life. That which is already true at the unseen level (heaven) is also manifesting at the level of the visible (earth).

This attitude allows you to take your focus off the limitations of the apparent problem and turn it to the limitless possibilities of Spirit. Spirit, as unformed, intelligent energy, is always looking for ways to express through specific channels. A seed you hold in your hand is endowed with this life, but it must be planted in a growing environment to begin its transformative process. Then this unseen life and intelligence, the kingdom of God, becomes evident. The expansive will of the creative life force manifests.

When you pray, always remember that you are not attempting to get God to act. You are agreeing to open yourself to the action of God.

The Prospering act of Forgiveness

Part 3 of 6

> Give us this day our daily bread, and forgive us our debts as we forgive our debtors.

It's interesting to note in this line that the fulfillment of our daily bread, our daily needs, is tied to the act of forgiveness. If you consider this prayer from the affirmative point of view, you might think of this line as saying, *my needs for today are met and all blocks to my greater good are removed as I release all resentments of the past.* These words depict both receptive and releasing attitudes of mind.

The receptive attitude is substantiated by the idea of God as the loving provider, a willing source of good. An attitude of release indicates that the key to a greater flow of good is your act of letting go of anything that blocks this flow. When you hold resentment for even the smallest offense, your thought and emotional energies accumulate around that offense, creating a blockage that hinders the free flow of the divine. It is like dropping a large rock in an irrigation ditch. Soon other debris catches on the rock, hampering the free-flow of water. Forgiveness is the equivalent of removing the rock and restoring the natural flow of life-giving water.

In another place, Jesus speaks of this dynamic in this slightly different way: *"So if you are offering your gift at the altar, and there remember that your brother or sister has something against you, leave your gift there before the altar and go; first be reconciled to your brother or sister, and then come and offer your gift."* (Matthew 5:23-24). It's all about keeping your mind an open channel through which the infinite life of God may manifest in continually expansive ways.

Charles Fillmore pointed out that mind is the "common meeting ground of God and man." When our mind is locked in resentment, our creativity and receptivity become restricted to a very narrow level of operation. This line in the *Lord's Prayer* reminds us to keep the avenue of mind open and fluid.

Freedom in Forgiveness

Part 4 of 6

Forgive us our debts as we forgive our debtors.

Because the act of forgiveness is so important, I want to elaborate on the subject.

When we think of the activity of God, we may be tempted to think that we have the power to influence the way God behaves. If we do the right thing, God will act favorably toward us. If we do the wrong thing, God will treat us differently. If God was an old man in the sky, this may be true. Jesus, however, illustrated in his parable of the prodigal son that God behaves the same always. The father in this parable never did anything but love and give to his wayward son. The son's actions, not the father's, caused the son's problems. Likewise, it was the son's actions that brought him back into alignment with a more prosperous life.

When you feel or even know with certainty that someone has harmed you, you take a mental and emotional position. This is a perspective that causes you to think, feel and act from this particular point of view. Your fixed point of view is your experience in life. The view from a mountaintop is much wider than the view from a canyon floor. Therefore, you have to ask yourself which view you desire to experience. The actions of another need not determine which view you hold. The view you hold is a choice you make.

Forgiveness is all about releasing one undesirable position (point of view) in favor of one that is desirable. Just because someone's words or actions appear to be out of integrity with spiritual principle does not mean that you are obligated to respond in kind. You do not have to condone their action, but duplicating it is no answer. Forgiveness lifts you from the common, reactive mode to the more effective position of initiating new and productive action. While you do not want to ignore your negative response to another, you do not want to allow their words and actions set the tone for your own. If you do, you will not rise above the level they represent. This is the key to finding freedom in forgiveness.

The Tempter Within

And leave us not in temptation, but deliver us from evil.

There are a number of versions of this line in the *Lord's Prayer*. The traditional version is, *And lead us not into temptation, but deliver us from evil.* The Aramaic version reads, *And let us not enter into temptation, but deliver us from evil.* The version I'm using is suggested by Charles Fillmore, who argued that the Lord would never lead us into temptation. Likewise, it is a bit awkward to think that if we succumbed to temptation, we could blame the Lord. *I asked you to make sure I didn't enter temptation, and here I am. Do you mind explaining why you let me do this?*

Again, if we take the affirmative approach to this line, we will find it a helpful reminder that our strength is always present, even in our weakest moments.

There are times when you feel flush with strength and optimism, when you know that you can move forward with confidence regardless of apparent obstacles. Then there are those times when the appearances get the best of you. You look out and survey the landscape of your life and you wonder why you ever thought you could succeed. At such moments, it is important to remember that God, your unfailing source of strength, power and wisdom, can never leave you.

The tempter within is not an entity that is trying to snare your soul and lead you to a path of self-destruction. It is that lesser self in you, that region of consciousness that does not grasp the fuller truth of the omnipresence of God. The word *evil* can be understood as error or erroneous thinking, thinking that is based on appearances and half-truths rather than on the truth of your wholeness and the potential that your life holds. Our conceptual translation of this line, therefore, would go something like this: *In my moments of weakness, your limitless love, power and wisdom lift me above all erroneous appearances.*

Making this inner shift connects you with your point of strength, and you again move forward in confidence and in peace.

One Presence, One Power

Part 6 of 6

For Thine is the kingdom, and the power, and the glory forever. Amen

This final line in the Lord's Prayer is the equivalent of saying, *There is but one presence and one power in the universe; God, the Good, omnipotent.* This is a fitting realization to hold for any prayer.

How many times have you prayed for some greater good in your life and then closed your prayer with the attitude, *I hope it works.* The closing line, which is not actually found in the Bible, is an affirmation that there are no blocks, no negative powers working against you. There is no reason to expect anything but the highest and the best outworking of the thing that concerns you. *Amen* is a seal of acceptance, an affirmation of *so be it,* or *so it is.* You could conceptually translate the line like this: *My greater good now unfolds completely unhindered in wonderful ways that work for the highest good of all, and I receive it now.*

One of the best ways to approach the idea of prayer is to think of it as a creative process. When you pray, you are opening yourself to God as a creative life force. You are planting a seed and agreeing to allow it to grow as a new condition in your life. When you plant a seed, you release it with the certain expectation that this tiny package of potential will produce in a certain way. You do not, however, meddle in the growing process. You trust and you keep the growing environment free of hindrances to its growth. The tiny sprout that first appears looks nothing like the full plant that you know is coming forth. This does not concern you because you know something good is happening, and you are patient and expectant with the growing process.

You and I do not have the power to influence the way God behaves. We do have the power to put ourselves in harmony with God's expansive behavior. We do this through the acceptance that the greater good we desire is now coming forth in perfect timing and in perfect order. And so it is.

The Lord's Prayer

Conceptual Summary

All-providing Source, ever expanding through me, wholeness is Your nature.

Your kingdom is present. Your will of absolute good is being done in my life as it is in Your unseen realm.

You are now imparting through me Your limitless substance.

I release all feelings of limitation, all resentments and all fear. I am free to move in new and prospering directions.

If I am tempted to judge by appearances of limitation, I remember Your freeing presence, and I am released from this error.

My greater good now unfolds completely unhindered in wonderful ways that work for the highest good of all.

I do receive it now.

A Quantum Leap of Faith

In an effort to better understand and grasp the abstract notion that the kingdom of God is within every individual, we can use the computer as a helpful model. We are trained from birth to think of ourselves in the same way we might think of our computer. The physical aspect is like the body, the processor is the brain or intellect. The software and all the data we generate and store on the hard drive would represent the consciousness. The hard drive is the storage facility, equivalent to the subconsciousness.

If you were to apply the pronoun *I* to this computer as a reference to its self-image, you would have the computer saying, *I am the sum of the physical and nonphysical aspects of this single unit.*

Taking a leap, let's say the kingdom of God is the *Internet*. If we said, the kingdom of the Internet is within our computer, are we saying that we could dismantle the computer and find a thing inside that we could identify as the Internet? We would have to say that the computer, through its internal modem, has the ability to access the Internet. Where is the Internet? Are we making a misleading statement by saying the kingdom of the Internet is within? No. The mistake we are making is in our belief that we are the computer.

In truth, our soul, our spiritual essence, that kingdom of God of which we speak, is the Internet. The computer is simply our means of making the invisible Internet visible at the material plane.

The Internet, in a sense, is omnipresent. You can access it in virtually any location. It remains invisible until there is a physical device, your computer, to make it visible. Your soul is exactly the same. Your mind and body are your soul's interface that enables you to interact and communicate at the physical level. It would be more accurate to think of your consciousness and your body existing within your soul, rather than the other way around.

While this may seem as if it takes a quantum leap of faith to grasp, I suggest you hold this thought for a time and see what other lights come on.

Demonstrating Prosperity

> I am the vine, you are the branches. He who abides in me, and I in him, he it is that bears much fruit.
>
> John 15:5

Few spiritually minded people would argue against the idea that God created us. How many stop to consider, however, that God is continuously creating us? If we see our creation as something that occurred in the past, that God formed us in the womb of our mother and sent us out into the cold world to fend for ourselves, we are cutting ourselves off from the key source of our spiritual and material supply.

In this fifteenth chapter of John, Jesus gives one of the most beautiful and simple metaphors for understanding God as our infinite supply. Our relationship to God is that of a vine and its branches. Those who live in vineyard country immediately see the picture. The vine grows from the earth and shoots out many branches. Cut the branch from the vine and the branch dies. It could say, "I was created from the vine," but being severed, we know that all growth stops. The branch that remains attached to the vine produces clusters of fruit.

To "abide in me" means to live with the awareness that your being arises from God, your living and present Source. The fruit represents all the various conditions of your life. The power to produce fruit does not originate in the branch. If it did, the branch would produce even though it was severed from the vine. You, the branch, are a channel through which God first diversifies in the material realm. The fruit is your channel through which you, the image and likeness of God, also diversify in the material realm. In other words, the conditions of your life are a continuation of the creative process of God. If your conditions seem meager and lacking, it is because you see yourself as something separate from your Source, the vine.

Visualize yourself as a branch. On one end, you are rooted in God, the life-giving vine. On the other end, you are producing clusters of fruit. In a working understanding of this relationship, the conditions of your life are the fruit and God is your source. You are transforming the Invisible into the visible.

Open your mind to this whole relationship. See it as a living reality and you will bear much fruit of a sweet and satisfying nature.

A Question of Faith

Faith is the substance of things hoped for, the evidence of things not seen.

– Hebrews 11:1

… faith takes right hold of the substance of the things desired, and brings into the world of evidence the things that before were not seen. … things that are seen are not made out of visible things, but out of the invisible. In some way, then, we understand that whatever we want is in this surrounding invisible substance, and faith is the power that can bring it out into actuality to us.

– Emilie Cady

To many, the word faith is associated with the religious beliefs held by an individual. Those beliefs, in turn, are attributed to a body of teachings known as Catholic and all its variations, Protestant and all its variations, Buddhist and all its variations, and so on. Cady treats faith, not as a body of religious ideas, but as a faculty of mind whose function is to translate the invisible into the visible.

The life we manifest is directly related to the way we use this faculty of faith. We may feel that we need more faith, but in truth, we need only learn to redirect our faith in the good we desire. We always have faith in something, and it's quite possible that we're using this faculty to bring forth conditions that are not to our liking.

Point a telescope to the ground and you will not see objects in the night sky. The telescope is not broken; it is simply pointed in the wrong direction. Point it to the heavens and you will see a very different world. The same is true with our faculty of faith.

One of the best ways to assure that our faith is pointed in the right direction is through creating affirmative statements that depict your desired good as a present reality. *God's wholeness now manifests as my perfect health* would be an example of turning our faith to healing. *God as my Source is now expressing as abundant supply* would be an example of turning our faith to prosperity. *God's perfect order now unfolds in my life*, points our faith in divine order.

As you speak your words, embrace them with the emotion that also affirms their truth. Feel as much as you envision your greater good coming forth. You don't need more faith; you only need to keep your faith pointed in the right direction.

Beyond the Dark Night of the Soul

> And going a little farther he fell on his face and prayed, "My Father, if it be possible, let this cup pass from me; nevertheless, not as I will, but as thou wilt.
>
> Matthew 26:39

Your spiritual awakening is a unique path that only you can walk. In the early stages, you are excited by the prospects of turning within and finding the inner, unfailing light that will guide you in all ways. In your progress, however, every one of your developing beliefs will be challenged, usually by some form of controversy. You are forced to decide what is true and what is not.

In this moving story, we find Jesus in one such moment. He is spending a sleepless night with his trusted circle of disciples, and yet he is very much alone. The disciples are exhausted and cannot stay awake to console their friend and leader. While Jesus expresses his disappointment in them, he knows he is confronted with something that only he can do, though with a great deal of trepidation. Twice more he prays, "My Father, if this cannot pass unless I drink it, thy will be done."

Jesus, like most of us, would draw strength from his friends. In their slumber, however, they are unable to offer him any support. He is forced to stand alone with his God, to completely surrender to the unfolding process of his own soul, despite the fact that the contents of the "cup" he must drink goes against every one of his natural survival instincts. Metaphorically, this is a battle between his emerging soul and the last vestiges of his senses-based self-image.

Life's meaning is not found in the acquisition of things, but in the bringing forth an awareness of the soul as our central identity. Every challenge provides an opportunity to let go of some belief that frustrates this awakening. We learn to trust, to surrender to the emerging new inspiration that is transforming the way we see and define ourselves. While this is not always a pleasant cup to drink, we are moving from an understanding of ourselves as a personal, limited ego to the universal being, the image and likeness of God that we truly are.

Yes, there will be dark and sleepless nights, but these are always followed by the bright and sunny morning of a new day full of promise.

Let There be Light

> The earth was without form and void, and darkness was upon the face of the deep; and the Spirit of God was moving over the face of the waters. And God said, 'Let there be light'; and there was light.
>
> – Genesis 1:2-3

When we read these familiar lines, our thoughts most likely shoot back to primordial times of our cosmic beginnings. We envision a state where things are just kind of there, a formless nothingness that is void of life, emotion and lacking any kind of meaningful and progressive activity.

For some, this chaotic state may be a more apt description of their current life. Things are just kind of there, a formless nothing about which they are not enthusiastic. It all seems to be just a meaningless panorama floating by. If you have such a life, these verses hold an important key for change.

Notice that nothing of the dark void changes until God speaks in a specific manner. By specific, I mean that God is neither describing nor complaining about the condition of the situation. God is not saying, "Look at this mess! Nothing makes any sense. Why am I here? Why do I bother?" To the contrary, God makes the affirmative statement, "Let there be light," and there is light.

It is doubtful that this ancient Hebrew writer held an accurate view of the literal beginnings of this universe. It is certain, however, that he had a clear view of the transformative principle of the spoken word.

Most of us are experts at describing negative conditions. We may even feel obligated to do so. After all, things are what they are. Why fool ourselves? Fortunately, one new idea, one new insight can change the way we see everything. One moment chaos can reign in our mind, and the next moment that chaos can become a field of infinite possibilities just waiting for us to sit up and take charge.

When spoken with the understanding that the full power of God is behind you, these simple words, *let there be light*, can provide a major catalyst for new opportunities and positive change. Instead of describing things as they appear to be, affirm, *let there be light*, and there will be light.

Choosing Your Vision

> Again, the kingdom of heaven is like a net which was thrown into the sea and gathered fish of every kind; when it was full, men drew it ashore and sat down and sorted the good into vessels but threw away the bad.
>
> Matthew 13:47-48

What is a "good" fish, and what is a "bad" fish? In the realm of the Divine, there is no such distinction. God is equally invested in the carp and the tuna. Determining the difference between a good fish and a bad fish depends on who is doing the determining. If you want fish you intend to sell through a pet store, you use one standard of judgment. If you are supplying a restaurant, you use another standard.

Your mind is like a net that you are constantly casting into the infinite sea of ideas. The ideas you bring in and keep, culminate as the conditions or tendencies reflected in and as your life. When you set a goal for yourself, your choice of the mental pictures and of the thoughts and feelings you hold about that goal become relevant. Excitement toward your objective becomes a good fish. Doubts in your abilities become bad fish. You want all the creative energy of your being to support your vision, so you make an effort to dismiss your doubts and reaffirm your excitement.

This principle holds true at all levels of action, not just mental and emotional. The activities you engage in, the conversations you conduct, the types of television programs you watch, the material you read all have their impact on the vision you desire to express. If you engage only in actions that support your vision, your vision will materialize. If you engage in actions that diminish your vision, you will get only a partial and inadequate demonstration.

The message of this parable is simple: Hold on to the ideas and actions that support your vision and let go of the ideas and actions that do not.

One Source

There is but one Source of being. This Source is the living fountain of all good, be it life, love, wisdom, power – the Giver of all good gifts. This source and you are connected, every moment of your existence. You have power to draw on this Source for all of good you are, or ever will be, capable of desiring.

— Emilie Cady

At first glance, it may be difficult to reconcile this statement with the fact that much of the good we desire seems to exist in the material realm. How can we draw material objects and conditions from an unseen inner Source? It is from within that we build the supportive consciousness and translate our desires into the forms we need.

Jesus specifically addressed the issue of material needs when he said,

> Do not be anxious about your life, what you shall eat or what you shall drink, nor about your body, what you shall put on. Is not life more than food, and the body more than clothing? Look at the birds of the air: they neither sow nor reap nor

gather into barns, and yet your heavenly Father feeds them. Are you not of more value than they? (Matthew 6:25-26).

This is a beautiful argument supporting the logic of trust in God. When you live with the attitude that it is not your own wisdom and intelligence that draws your good, but the wisdom and intelligence of God, you live in faith that the things you need will appear at the right time, in the right way and without making the pursuit of these things the object of your existence.

As Cady says, every person is connected to his or her one Source every moment. This means if our back is up against a wall, there is a way out. The life, love, power and intelligence of God is at work at this very moment to open new doors, present new opportunities, and inspire each of us with new and creative insight.

Giving Up Means Giving Way

> After these things God tested Abraham, and said to him, 'Abraham!' And he said, 'Here am I.' He said, 'Take your son, your only son Isaac, whom you love, and go to the land of Mori'ah, and offer him there as a burnt offering upon one of the mountains of which I shall tell you.'
>
> Genesis 22:1-2

While we may be repulsed and tempted to dispose of stories like this as irrelevant, we would be tossing out the proverbial baby with the bathwater. From a metaphysical point of view, this episode from the life of Abraham is filled with meaning that you and I can use in our own spiritual unfolding.

Abraham is being asked by the Lord to give up the most important thing in his life – his only son. He is prepared to do it, but then he discovers that he does not have to, that there is another alternative. He may sacrifice a nearby ram instead. So what could this possibly mean to us?

Animals represent a strong level of material thought within our consciousness. The sacrifice of animals in the Bible should be thought of, not as a way of appeasing a capricious god, but as a letting go of our strong attachment to the material realm as the source of our happiness and well-being.

In the story, Abraham is asked to sacrifice his son, but then is given the alternative of sacrificing the ram instead. The metaphysical gem here is this: The things we cherish most become the source of our identity, our happiness and well being. Spiritually speaking, however, we have one Source, one internal fountain from which all the good we can possibly desire flows forth. Happiness is not found in things; it is a state of alignment with our eternal Source. As this internal alignment occurs, we bring the upwelling joy into all we do. Where joy and enthusiasm are present, there is success. Barriers fall and obstacles become opportunities for more success.

Giving up, that is, the willingness to sacrifice our attachment to things as the source of our power is the means of giving way to that higher power of wisdom and intelligence to unfold through us. Like Abraham, we lose nothing by letting go but instead gain the fulfillment of the promise of unlimited expression.

What is Greater Good?

Recently I was involved in a conversation with a colleague who raised the question of what we mean by the term, *greater good*. It's a very good question. When we ask it of ourselves, and we are honest, we consider the difference between what we think we want and what is actually the best outworking of a given situation.

Some years ago an elderly woman who had, for years, struggled with failing health, asked me if I thought it was okay for her to let go and move one. "I'm so tired," she said. "I see no point fighting to stay in the body. My whole family is praying for me to be healed. I think the healing I need is to let go of this broken body."

From the family's point of view, *greater good* was defined as keeping their mother in her body. From her point of view, she was ready to do exactly the opposite and let go. Which one was right? If you could play the role of God for a moment, which prayer would you answer? The family was obviously reluctant to experience of loss of their loved one. Who can blame them? But were they thinking of their highest good, or were they thinking of the highest good for their mother? They were willing to set aside her wishes for their own. If their prayer truly were for their mother's highest good, then they would let go of their preconceived ideas, listen to their mother and release her from their personal wishes.

We have all prayed for specific outcomes to troubling situations. Have we not also observed these situations working out, but not in ways we wanted or expected? We naturally arrive at specifics based on our understanding of a given situation. Do we know all the facts? Do we see the situation from the all-knowing perspective of divine wisdom?

Our best approach is to feel free to name the greater good, but to do so with the condition, *this or something better*. Something better, however, may be exactly the opposite of what we think is best. The mother passed within two weeks of our visit. As expected, the family was devastated, their pain compounded by their inability to accept their mother's interpretation of greater good.

This is a great reminder if you are praying for the right outworking of a situation. Do not be afraid to name the greater good you desire, but let your definition be expansive enough to include *this, or something better*.

How to Let Go

> Do you not believe that I am in the Father and the Father in me? The words that I say to you I do not speak on my own authority; but the Father who dwells in me does his works.
>
> – John 14:10

Imagine that I hold in my hand a tiny acorn. I announce that I have heard this acorn can become a mighty oak tree, but I am not sure how this is possible. I know the oak tree needs roots, that it has a trunk, branches and many leaves. Therefore, I appoint four committees. There is the root committee, the trunk committee, the branch committee and the leaf committee. We then begin the process of discussing all the things we should do to bring forth an oak tree. After lengthy discussion, we develop a plan and begin dissecting the acorn. We find there is an embryonic representation of the tree within that seed. Each committee then studies its respective components, carefully removes the embryonic tree, and places it, roots first, in soil.

Can you see any ways that the concept of letting go might apply in this scenario? First, do we need the expertise of four committees to make an oak tree happen? No. We can let that go. Do we need to understand how the invisible life energy interacts with the physical seed to make an oak tree happen? No. We can let that go. After some serious deliberation, we will likely conclude that all we need to do is drop the acorn into soil. Now, a soil amending committee might be good. This committee could actually do something useful by creating a rich environment that will nourish our acorn. It might also provide some periodic watering and further nutrients if needed.

We have let go, not of our desire to manifest an oak tree, but of the impossibly huge responsibility of making it grow.

Letting go is the process of creating the environment out of which your desires may naturally manifest. If you will let go of your need to create the world of your dreams and focus instead on allowing your free and limitless soul to emerge, you will discover that your life, like the oak tree, begins unfolding in stress-free, balanced and perfectly prosperous ways.

Guidance

We are spiritual beings who have, for reasons we know at the deepest level, stepped into this earthly experience to accomplish some work important to us. We brought with us our connection to our eternal source of guidance and supply, a resource of wisdom and guidance that will always lead us to the right answers when we need them.

Run To, Not From

> It is perfectly natural for the human mind to seek to escape from its troubles by running away from present environments, or by planning some change on the material plane. There is no permanent or real outward way of escape from miseries or circumstances; all help must come from within.
>
> – Emilie Cady

Most of us have dreams and desires that would have us leaving one condition and moving to another. While the motivation for some of these changes may seem obvious – simple improvements to our life conditions – others may be pointing to our need to be still and take another look. We might be running from an inner call to come up higher, to begin filling from within the undesired condition we hope to escape.

We usually see unsatisfying conditions as a glass filled only half way with water. We want a full glass and so we set aside the half-empty glass and pursue one that is fuller. Rather than set the half-filled glass aside, it may be that we simply need to fill the glass we have rather than seek another.

When Cady suggests that help must come from within, she is pointing to the idea of beginning right where we are, using the conditions we have, to begin filling our life. In other words, rather than curse our conditions, we start blessing them and asking how we can give more of ourselves to fill them.

You may be in a demanding relationship and you say, "I'm already giving as much as I can, and they just keep wanting more." Maybe you are feeling drained, not because you are giving so much, but because you are giving against your will. If you want to fill this glass, you have to stop denying how you really feel and begin giving from a basis that is true. You are going along to get along, so you're not really giving out of who you are, and the relationship suffers because of it.

Pour the full force of your being into your present circumstances. Top off the cup that is yours to fill. When it is full, you may decide you want to keep it.

Living Your Truth

A man went out to plant, and some of his seed fell along the path and was quickly eaten by birds. Other seed fell among rocks where there wasn't much soil. The seed sprang up quickly, but because there was a lack of soil, it did not root properly and the young plants were quickly scorched to death by the sun. Other seed fell among weeds, and the weeds robbed it of nutrients so it yielded no grain. Still other seed fell in good soil, and it grew well, yielding great abundance.

Paraphrase of Mark 4:3-9

 This is a parable of spiritual ideas and their reaction to various types of consciousness. Let's say someone makes the statement, "*You are an expression of the Infinite and you can do whatever you want with your life.*" One person will like what they hear but then go about their life, business as usual. This is the first condition of consciousness, where the seed is snatched up quickly by birds. The second condition is one that hears the statement through a mind so full of preconditioned ideas of lack and self-doubt (rocky soil) that it can take no root in their thinking. The third example hears the statement, but their mind is so consumed with the chores of daily living (weeds) that this new idea receives no serious consideration and, therefore, has no influence in their thinking. The last example represents a state of consciousness that takes the idea seriously and begins the process of measuring everything it believes against this new benchmark.

This is an excellent explanation of why there can be such varied levels of experience among the human species. The range between poverty and opulence is wide. The interesting point to observe, however, is that this vast range of discrepancy does not exist in any other species but the human, and this parable explains why. We possess a creative mind, a faculty of imagination, and we alone can decide how we use it.

James suggested that we become more than "hearers of the word." He said we must become "doers," to seek to live the truth we know.

Seeing is Believing

> Everything undesirable passes away if we refuse absolutely to give it recognition by word, deed, or thought as a reality. This we can the more easily do when we remember that nothing is real except the eternal.
>
> – Emilie Cady

The above passage, which I quoted in an earlier article, reminds me of the philosophical theme of Heraclites. He pointed out that everything is in a state of flux, that you can't step twice into the same river. Life is a flowing dynamic whose natural tendency is to carry away all that is not grounded in its changeless reality. This includes every negative accumulation of thought and circumstance that contribute to our experience. All that is required on our part is a willingness to let go.

When we latch on to a negative appearance through our word, deed, and thought we actually expand on and give substance to the appearance. A single log can lodge in a stream and cause a buildup of rubble. This blockage restricts the flow of the stream and may create a stagnant pool where fresh water once flowed. When we hold on to a negative appearance, a "pool" of thought and emotion build up behind it, and we find ourselves literally swimming in a stagnated backup of energy.

The natural remedy to a stream's blockage is a flash flood, nature's way of clearing its clogged arteries. With us, it is unnecessary to experience a flash flood because we have the capacity to dismantle this emotional blockage through a conscious effort of letting go. As Cady suggests, it becomes much easier to let go when we realize the thing we are hanging onto is temporal, that the eternal qualities of prosperity, peace, love, and balance will flow naturally into our experience the moment we clear the way through releasing.

Are you swimming in a pool of negativity? Decide today to start letting go of your hold on negative appearances. Dislodge that log of negative emotion that keeps your life from flowing freely. Only the eternal is real and satisfying. Let go and let the eternal heal your life.

The Invincible Spirit

> For truly I say to you, if you have faith as a grain of mustard seed, you will say to this mountain, 'Move from here to there,' and it will move; and nothing will be impossible to you.
>
> Matthew 17:20

While the challenges of life will try to convince us otherwise, there is within each one of us an invincible spirit. A part of us knows no fear, no defeat, no limitation and no uncertainty about our future. The spiritual dimension is an irrepressible force of eternal life that rises from the depths of our infinite nature.

Does something stand in the way of your good? Then pause to remember that God is the source of your being. God is your wisdom, your strength, your invincible spirit. This thing cannot stand for long. There is a way around it, over it, or through it and the wisdom of God will show you that way.

Do you have a dream that seems to lie just out of your reach? Then know that God's infinite spirit in you knows how to make that dream a reality. Yours is a spirit of enthusiasm, of responsiveness, of clarity, of patience. Yours is an invincible spirit.

Is your body failing to show the health and vitality that are rightfully yours? Affirm that your invincible spirit is now bubbling forth as new health and vibrant life. Speak healing words to your body. Hold the vision of what you want, not what you do not want for the physical level of your being.

Your consciousness is the gate through which God's limitless life makes its appearance in the world as you. You open this gate through understanding that greater levels of living are possible to you now because you are connected to the Infinite.

Affirm: *The invincible spirit of God manifests through every aspect of my mind, body and affairs. There are no obstacles in my life. There is only God.*

You are the invincible spirit of God in expression. Let this be the standard from which you view your world.

The Faith Factor

"... faith takes right hold of the substance of the things desired, and brings into the world of evidence the things that before were not seen. Further speaking of faith, the writer [of Hebrews] said, "Things which are seen were not made of things which do appear;" that is, things that are seen are not made out of visible things, but out of the invisible. In some way, then, we understand that whatever we want is in this surrounding invisible substance, and faith is the power that can bring it out into actuality to us."

— Emilie Cady

In all spiritually based literature, we find significant discussion on the importance of faith. Spiritual pioneers like Emilie Cady sought to take our understanding of faith beyond a simple belief in God, important as this is, to an understanding of how our faculty of faith actually works. She agrees with the writer of Hebrews that we are all equipped with this faculty that brings conditions and things into visibility. Our entire life condition is, in fact, the effect of our exercise of faith.

When you think of your life, do you do so with some measure of dread, or do you have a good feeling that things are unfolding in a positive and progressive way? Is your faith invested in greater good emerging, or are you plagued with doubts that this is true? In other words, what are you expecting from your life? Observe the tendencies of your expectations and you'll understand how you are employing your faculty of faith.

Where is my faith? What are my expectations? These are good questions to ask yourself both in critical moments and as you go through your day. The writer of Hebrews pointed out that faith is the substance of things hoped for, the evidence of things not seen. The key is to become aware of what it is we are hoping for, and what we are actually expecting.

Today, turn the power of your faith on the greater good you want to unfold in your life. Get the feeling that this good is now coming forth, that your life is successful and prosperous in all ways. Be steady in your faith in the good and give thanks that it is now coming forth.

The Intuitive Voice

In the spiritual context, one of the most important aspects to understand is that of intuition. I think I can also add that this is one of the most difficult to explain. The reason is difficult is that our normal mode of learning is through our senses-based intellect. You are using your eyes to read this message and you are processing the information, but this doesn't assure that you will experience any kind of spiritual transformation.

Intuitive knowing is a direct and conscious experience of your spiritual essence. Though this spiritual essence is universal, present in every person and every living creature, few people actually know it as a first-hand experience. We have formed mental images of our spiritual nature and we freely use the term without actually experiencing the reality behind the idea.

Imagine looking at a photograph of a sun-drenched meadow. Then think of a time when you were actually in such a meadow. The sights, sounds, air, warmth of the sun and the feel of the earth beneath your feet all give you something a photo cannot.

Why is it important to consciously experience our spiritual essence? Because all the qualities we seek in our spiritual quest are being pressed in upon us now. When you sit in the sun-drenched meadow, you receive the direct experience of everything this place has to give. You don't have to imagine anything. Likewise, a direct experience of your spiritual essence imparts the peace, balance, inspiration and harmony that you are looking for. These qualities begin to integrate into your thinking. Your mind opens to new possibilities and new standards for experiencing your world. In short, an eternal element is introduced into your awareness.

The intuitive voice is not an audible voice. It is a direct impartation of the presence of God. Just as every person is capable of experiencing directly all the beauty of the meadow, so each is capable of consciously experiencing the living presence of God. Nothing will bring more balance to your life than this.

The Storm Will Pass

Everyone then who hears these words of mine and does them will be like a wise man who built his house upon the rock; and the rain fell, and the floods came, and the winds blew and beat upon that house, but it did not fall, because it had been founded on the rock. And every one who hears these words of mine and does not do them will be like a foolish man who built his house upon the sand; and the rain fell, and the floods came, and the winds blew and beat against that house, and it fell; and great was the fall of it"

> Matthew 7:24-27

When a storm moves into our life, we may be tempted to reel and spend a lot of time questioning why it is happening. One of the strengths of Jesus as a minister was his ability to say, "Life is not always easy; it will throw you some curves. And when it does, here is the way to handle it." I have the feeling that if Jesus drove a car, he'd have a bumper sticker that said, *"Storms Happen!"*

We're most affected, not by the surface storms, but by the mental and emotional uncertainty that rages through our mind while trying to find some anchor to keep us steady. That anchor is our inner connection with God, the source of all our strength and assurance.

Every storm in life reveals an interesting dynamic in our consciousness. Something occurs that appears to be out of our control, so we try to fix it. When we realize we can't fix it, we enlist the help of all our external resources. When the storm continues to rage, we begin to feel panic, maybe even overwhelmed. If we continue approaching the storm as an external problem only, our house, our peace of mind, our inner sense of security will collapse.

Taking the time to turn within and reconnect with our Source, however, will allow us to watch the storm from a secure shelter. It's the difference in being caught in a storm while hiking as opposed to enjoying it from the safety of your front porch.

If your life is stormy right now, take time to reconnect with that rock-solid part of yourself. The storm, as always, will pass.

Navigating Through Illusion

There is a way which seems right to a man, but its end is the way to death.

— Proverbs 14:12

If you trace to its source the weight of the world that you carry in your thought and emotion, you will not find it bubbling forth from the conditions about which you are thinking. You will find this weight rising from an out-of-control imagination.

Most of the things that capture our imagination in a negative way do not exist. We take a bit of information that may or may not be true, and we run with it into all kinds of scenarios that have nothing to do with what is actually happening. It's what *might* happen that occupies our minds. Then, as if we're not good enough at sending our imagination down peace-destroying paths, we watch sensationalized news reports and crime dramas so we can experience vicariously the problems of others, to give our imaginations some genuine material over which to worry.

A certain mindset claims it is the obligation of each individual to keep up with what's happening in the world. Do we not also have some sense of obligation to keep up with what's happening beneath the surface appearances and interpretations of those whose sole intention is to seize our imagination?

If you would find inner peace and security, one of your first steps is deciding who and what is in charge of your imagination. If it's not you, then your problems will persist. All bodily stress is the direct effect of this undisciplined faculty. Until you begin saying "no" to the wild rides, the fear-filled what ifs, the tantrums of self-pity, the contemplation of all the perceived things you believe you lack in life or simply the idle preoccupation with useless information you will never attain the inner quality of life that you crave.

Make the decision to put a bit in the mouth of your imagination, insisting that it take you where you want to go. It is a very willing and faithful servant and it is waiting for you, the master of your household, to show up and give orders.

Losing and Living?

> He who finds his life will lose it, and he who loses his life for my sake will find it.
>
> – Matthew 10:39

I once read an article about a Christian missionary who was killed while spreading the "Word" in the Congo. The article included this saying of Jesus, indicating that the missionary's service to the Christian cause guaranteed him a place in Heaven.

Is this what Jesus had in mind with this paradoxical statement? Certainly, the historical record provides justification for such an interpretation, for many early Christians lost their lives practicing their religion. This persecution, however, did not begin until after the death of Jesus. There is much evidence to suggest that he referred to a metaphorical rather than a literal death in this saying.

The life we have found and live is one that is based largely on the perception of the senses. We evaluate things based on our experience rather than on our limitless, spiritual potential. When we say, "I can't do this thing," we are speaking from the life we have "found," something that is now part of our past.

The suggestion in this saying is that we can find a new way to experience life that is based more on our limitless potential than on our past. Finding this new basis requires a giving up of the old. Losing is not really losing, but more of a transforming from an old state to a new, much as the caterpillar transforms into a butterfly. The insect loses its earthbound identity, but gains a freedom unknown in the caterpillar world.

Are you currently earthbound, restricted by unwanted conditions and relationships? Instead of lamenting your condition, enter quiet moments in which you stop fighting and let go. In these introspective times, let your goal become a process of *dying* to your suffering self. Are you worrying about something? Die to your worry. Feel the strength of knowing your butterfly self is emerging, that a completely new way of experiencing life is evolving from the shell of your former self.

God does not judge you by past performance, but gives you as much life as you are willing to take. Lose the old, and begin to live.

In Harmony with God

You and I do not have the power to influence the way God behaves.
We do, however, have the power to put ourselves in harmony with God's expansive behavior.

The Whole Picture

Suppose that a dozen persons are standing on the dark side of a wall in which are various sized openings. Viewing the scene outside through the opening assigned to him, one sees all there is within a certain radius. He says, "I see the whole world; in it are trees and fields." Another, through a larger opening, has a more extended view; he says: "I see trees and fields and houses; I see the whole world." The next one, looking through a still larger opening, exclaims: "Oh! You are all wrong! I alone see the whole world; I see trees and fields and houses and rivers and animals. The fact is, each one looking at the same world sees according to the size of the aperture through which he is looking, and he limits the world to just his own circumscribed view of it.

– Emilie Cady

In this passage, Cady gives one of the best explanations as to why people see things so differently. From this illustration, we can also see why those who have had some measure of a spiritual awakening (have peeked over the fence) are reluctant to engage in proselytizing.

Each of us is looking at the world through the aperture of ideas we hold. What seems perfectly clear to one may not even register as significant with another, and vise versa. The important thing to remember is that we see the world, not as it is (without a fence), but as we are (through a hole).

If we do not like the world we see, our first consideration should be the size hole through which we are looking. If we are seeing and feeling restriction, we are looking through a very small hole. We take time to let go of our perspective so we can see through another, larger, hole. The time comes when we rise above the wall altogether, or at least we come to know the difference between peering through a small opening and seeing with clear spiritual vision.

I am grateful for people like Emilie Cady who have helped me come to know there is a difference between what is, and what I think is. Am I seeing the Whole or am I looking through a hole? When things are not looking so good, this is a good question to ask.

The Forgiveness Dynamic

Suppose you are the pilot of a hot-air balloon. You have so many bags of sand ballast on board that your balloon cannot take off the ground. You know you have to release some of your ballast. This will not be a problem unless you have a special interest in hanging onto your sand. If this is the case, you will have to decide if you want to keep your sand or fly.

This is a very simple way of illustrating the forgiveness dynamic. Each of us is endowed with the desire to be free, to fly. Our desire arises from the limitless life of God pressing out through us. Allowing this energy free reign will ultimately manifest as freedom in our circumstances. Like the balloon, we are lifted from conditions of limitation to conditions more fitting to our soul's natural state of freedom.

The ballast we carry is the mental and emotional energy that keeps us locked in a static state. This energy often takes the form of resentment toward another or even disappointment with our own actions or reactions. Forgiveness is the act of releasing this negative energy. The difficulty we have with letting go of such feelings is our tendency to personalize the incidents that triggered them. We go beyond asking why he or she did this thing, to why he or she did it to us. What right did they have?

While on one level we may find justification for reacting in anger and even holding resentment, it really comes down to the question of whether we want to cling to our sandbags of non-forgiveness, or if we want to let them go and fly.

Forgiveness is not casting a blind eye on the irresponsible actions of another or ignoring the need for accountability from those who have hurt us. Problems of a different sort can develop when we internalize and suppress such things. We are on our way to forgiveness, however, the moment we know that our peace and integrity are not dependent on the words and actions of another. Our power comes from within.

Though we may struggle to reach this point, we will do so because we gradually place more value on flying than on clinging to our bags of sand. The higher we rise, the better we see and the easier it is to let go.

The False Prophet

> False Christs and false prophets will arise and show signs and wonders, to lead astray, if possible, the elect.
>
> Mark 13:22

With all of the turmoil that we see in the world today, I was asked to comment on whether or not we might be in the end times as predicted in the Bible. Though it is commonly done, it is a mistake to use the Bible to support the notion of the end of the world or to think of it as a prophetic guide to the discernment of events leading to this disastrous conclusion. Respected theologians have been doing this for centuries, all without success. Biblical predictions of doom and end times must be understood from within the historical context in which they were written. They are nearly always intended as messages of hope for a people who were under persecution at the time the writing.

I think it is safe to say, however, that each one of us, in some degree, inhabits a world we hope will end. It is a world where we are not quite at peace. Perhaps we are struggling with meaning, or our ability to enjoy the present is hindered by concerns for the future.

There is a kind of prophet in us that predicts that someday this world will end. But before it does, certain things must happen. What things? You can make your list by finishing this sentence: I will be at peace when _____.

You might say you'll be at peace when your soul is mature enough to experience God at all times. You may be hoping for the day when your money issues are all resolved, or when you get a better paying job that you love. Maybe you're looking for the right person, or you are seeking to improve or regain your health. Perhaps you're waiting for some crisis to be brought to a successful conclusion.

Let's say in six months all of your stated conditions come to pass. What you will find is that peace still eludes you. Chances are good that the only thing that will change is the content of your list.

The false prophet in us is always telling us that the peace we crave is futuristic and conditional. Something on the outside must change before we can experience peace. You notice, however, that when this something changes, something else takes its place. Like a hamster running on a wheel, we're going through the motions but we get off this wheel in the same cage.

We silence the false prophet by entering quiet times with the full intention of opening our mind to our soul. There will always be issues to resolve, but doing so does not bring the peace that is ours at the spiritual level. Contrary to the insistence of our false prophet, nothing in our external world has to change to access this peace.

Take time daily to let go of all appearances in your life, turn your attention to the inner, natural radiance of your soul. As you consciously touch this spiritual wholeness, you will experience the peace you seek and you will carry it into every aspect of your life. Your tumultuous world will indeed come to an end, but it will do so in a very gentle and pleasing way.

This Too Shall Pass

All of us have been through challenging periods, some we readily remember and some we have forgotten. The challenge that reigns most prominently, of course, is the one we are facing today. Because of its seemingly endless demands on our attention, it is easy to forget that *this too shall pass*. Think of a former, all-consuming challenge that felt as if it would never end. The fact that you are thinking about it as a thing of the past shows that it did indeed come to pass.

On the stage of life, there is always some drama playing out. Each has its beginning, middle and end. From a spiritual perspective, it's important to remember that the one thing that does not change through it all is God. God, your all-sustaining source, is the same now as ever. The peace you crave is present. The freedom you desire is not dependent on the conclusion of the current scene. Yes, you want your present challenge to successfully resolve, but you also want the assurance now that it is in the process of passing. The only sure way to know this is to open your mind and heart to God.

Totally consumed with a challenge, it is easy to develop tunnel vision, a single way of seeing the collection of facts that stand before us. All great inventors, artists and leaders have not ignored negative facts, but have made the choice to see beyond them in ways that allow the further expression of new possibilities. The facts of a situation rarely represent the truth. Life is not the stagnant pool of problems it sometimes appears to be. There is always a new opening, a new idea, a different way of thinking and an inspired way of seeing things.

Take time to be still, to turn your attention away from your challenge and refocus on the ever-present help of God. Do not struggle with finding solutions. Solutions will find you, probably in quiet, unassuming changes you hardly notice. Know the wisdom of God is now working through you in beautiful and productive ways. Above all, know that this too shall pass.

Letting Go of the Old

> No one puts a piece of unshrunk cloth on an old garment, for the patch tears away from the garment, and a worse tear is made. Neither is new wine put into old wineskins; if it is, the skins burst, and the wine is spilled, and the skins are destroyed; but new wine is put into fresh wineskins, and so both are preserved.
>
> Matthew 9:16-17

In these two parables, Jesus furnishes us with a graphic illustration of a very important, freeing dynamic: the action of letting go. It is one thing to retain information for present and future use. It would be cumbersome if we had to re-learn to drive our car every time we got in. If, however, we dredged up the memory of a past auto accident every time we sat in our car, our paranoia may hinder our present driving performance.

If you carry old wounds into a new day, you will prevent yourself from seeing and experiencing the potential for new avenues of creative opportunity. Jesus said to let the dead bury the dead, and let the challenges of this day be the ones we give our full attention. How much of our creative energy is drained away replaying old hurts and dredging up old things we should or should not have said or done?

The full action of God is present in each new moment. Created in the image and after the likeness of God, each one of us is intended to bring the full force of our creative energy to bear on the things we have to do each day. We say we do not have enough time or energy to do what we would really like to do. How does God attend the minutest detail of this vast universe? By being fully present in each new moment.

Fortunately, you and I do not have the responsibility of running the universe. All we are expected to do is live our lives successfully. We can learn from God by being present in this now moment, by giving our attention to present tasks and letting go of the problems about which we can do nothing. The imagery of new wine and new wineskins is a great reminder when we are tempted to dredge up past failures and old wounds.

Who is in Charge?

If you would find inner peace and security, one of your first steps is deciding who and what is in charge of your imagination. If it's not you, then your problems will persist.

The Call

Sometime, somewhere, every human being must come to himself. Having tired of eating husks, he will 'arise and go to my Father.'

— Emilie Cady

Quoting from the parable of the prodigal son given by Jesus, Cady is stating an encouraging truth. The life many of us are living is likely but a representational fraction of the life that is trying to express itself through us. We sense the call to arise, to come up higher, and we translate this call into a vision of better, more freeing external conditions. The conditions we envision, however, may not be the true reflections of what God has in store for us. We are responding to the inner calling but we may not be fully surrendering to it.

Acknowledging that you are being called by God is the first and most important step toward the life you seek. Many do not realize that their desire for a freer life is really the expansive nature of God seeking to outpicture through them. By holding the thought that our desire for freedom is a product of personal ambition rather than a divine movement, we restrict the universal flow of greater good to a personal vision that will not exceed our senses-based understanding.

It is important to spend quality time laying aside all personal imagery of what we think our life can or should become and meditate on the inner call to *arise*. Jesus reminded us that it is the Father's good pleasure to give us the kingdom. The giving of this kingdom is not an act that will begin once we prove to God we are worthy of receiving. It has already begun. Our job is to learn how to receive it in its unconditional, unrestricted form.

In your quiet time, focus on your inner urge for a better life knowing this urge is the voice of God drawing you up to a free and satisfying experience. The attitude of surrender will free you from the tendency to tell God what you need or want and will align your thoughts with the higher purpose. As you go about your day, affirm something like, *"Thy will is now being done,"* and know that everyone and everything is coming into alignment with this inner calling.

Transcending the Law of Karma

> Think not that I have come to abolish the law and the prophets; I have come not to abolish them but to fulfill them.
>
> Matthew 5:17

The law and the prophets, that body of Old Testament rules that included the books of Moses and the compiled writings of ancient Israel's greatest seers, might be succinctly summarized as, *an eye for an eye and a tooth for a tooth*. Put in terms of everyday language, we might say that our life is as it is because we, somewhere along the line, have instigated a cause that created the effect.

There can be little doubt that our thoughts and actions are integral components to the conditions that surround us. The problem with karma, however, is that it leaves the believer rather powerless to do much of anything about his or her life. Many people labor beneath the weight of past *sins*, seeing the limiting conditions of their lives as the exact payment for something they must have done.

The concept of karma is rooted in the principle of *cause and effect*. What we do not always realize is that every moment we are creating a new cause. Each attitude we hold is the cause of some effect. Assuming the attitude that you are paying for past mistakes is, in fact, a cause that perpetuates the level of life you would rather leave behind.

Your consciousness bears the same relationship to your life that a rheostat has with the level of light in a room. Turn up the rheostat halfway, and you get a half lighted room. Turn it even more, and you get brighter light. You are not bound by a past setting of the rheostat. You always have at your fingertips the ability to initiate a new effect.

At any moment, you can begin to turn up the rheostat of your consciousness and experience more light and success in your life. You do not break any spiritual laws by letting go. You fulfill the law of cause and effect by consciously creating a new cause that will produce a desired effect.

Events and Experience

When you are working to change your life using spiritual principles, it is helpful to remember the significant difference between an event and an experience. An event is a thing that happens. An experience is what you do mentally and emotionally with what happens. The event is an external action. The experience you have is a composite of your imagination and your emotional reaction.

Let's say that you are walking down the sidewalk next to an elderly man and he steps into a pothole, loses his balance and falls. You help him get up and on his way, and you go your way. The event will cause you to have a certain kind of mental and emotional experience. Now suppose this elderly man is your father. It's the same type of event, but you have a very different kind of inner experience.

We spend a lot of time trying to manipulate our events so they will produce a more favorable experience. Our spiritual studies, however, reveal that approaching any challenge from the reverse is actually the most effective. We can't always change the event, but we always have something to say about how we will experience the event. We can recoil in fear when things seem to be falling apart, or we can declare that a greater good is unfolding through the apparent chaos.

When Jesus explained that his kingdom was not of this world, I believe he was talking about the world of events. He was not a master manipulator of events, but he had mastered the realm of his own inner experience. He was able to calm a stormy sea because he had already achieved an inner calm.

If you have been trying to change life at the event level so you can improve the quality of your inner experience, start today to reverse this process. As you think of the various things you would like to change, allow yourself to calmly achieve a level of peace about the appearance. Begin to give thanks that unseen good is now emerging through the event. Embrace the truth that this event is full of countless possibilities, and that you are not restricted to experiencing it in only one way. When you change your experience, you will master the event.

View From the Rim

> I lift up my eyes ...
>
> Psalms 121

A number of years ago, Beth and I took our two children on a vacation that included a trip to the *Grand Canyon*. While there, we made the spontaneous decision to hike *Bright Angel Trail*. Three hours and six miles later, we reached *Plateau Point*, still 800 feet above the *Colorado River*. By then we were already feeling exhaustion, so we did not go on down to the canyon floor. Putting it mildly, the hike back to the rim turned into a grueling, nine-hour test of endurance.

Depending on my location, my attitude toward the canyon shifted dramatically. From the rim, I found myself gazing awestruck into a breathtaking wonder. Photographs of the canyon abound, and many have tried to capture in writing the feelings induced by this natural phenomenon. None has been able to convey what I felt while staring into that vast chasm.

From the trail, both the view and my feelings were quite different. Without the perspective from the rim, we could have been in any canyon in the southwest. With the temperature topping a whopping 103 degrees, that hike became an uphill struggle through a fiery inferno, not quite as inspiring as the view from the rim.

On our hike through life, we can sometimes become so involved in the short-term struggles that we forget the larger spiritual context in which we live. We define ourselves as struggling little people rather than remembering that we are expressions of the Infinite. We may ask *why we are here*. What do we mean by *here*? Are we referring to our current struggle, or to the fact that we are hiking in one of the grandest natural wonders on earth?

It is very therapeutic for us to re-experience often our view from the rim, to let go of the immediate concerns of the hike and gaze out over the vastness that is our spiritual journey. For some, life has become a constant uphill struggle through an energy-draining inferno. For others, every day presents an exciting opportunity to experience yet another facet of this natural wonder that is our sojourn on earth.

Take time to sit quietly and open yourself to the view from the rim. It will give you an important sense of context that you simply cannot achieve while plodding along the trail, wishing you were elsewhere.

What You See is What You Get

> The kingdom of God is as if a man should scatter seed upon the ground, and should sleep and rise night and day, and the seed should sprout and grow, he knows not how. The earth produces of itself, first the blade, then the ear, then the full grain in the ear. But when the grain is ripe, at once he puts in the sickle, because the harvest has come.
>
> Mark 4:26-29

The people of Jesus' day, many of whom made their living in agriculture, would have needed no lesson in seed germination and growth. A deeper understanding of how to better one's life through spiritual awareness, on the other hand, was as much needed then as it is now.

Jesus was explaining that the kingdom of God, like the invisible force that grows the seed, is an expansive energy that is fully functioning, day and night, even as we sleep. He was telling his listeners that they could utilize this creative energy to grow a better life. Their decision to do so would begin with a vision of the type crop they wanted. This vision would be followed by the action of planting the appropriate seed.

The role of vision in our selection of seed determines how we engage the creative life force. Emma Curtis Hopkins pointed to this important fact when, commenting on our inner, visional sense, she wrote,

> "For it is primarily what we most see, and not what we most think, that constitutes our presence, power and history."

In terms of our life's direction, what we *see* is what we get. Our choice of the kinds of thought and feeling seeds we sow is determined by the direction our inner, visional sense is pointed most of the time. The creative life force itself is completely indifferent to the kinds of seeds we scatter. As we sleep through the night and move through the day, our seeds grow, we know not how.

Your life will change for the better to the degree that you see yourself as you are in truth: a pure, unadulterated expression of God. When you hold this true vision, your thoughts follow and your life changes to match your inner vision, first the blade, then the ear, then the full grain in the ear. What you see is what you get.

What's in Your House?

And Elisha said to her, 'What shall I do for you? Tell me; what have you in the house?' And she said, 'Your maidservant has nothing in the house, except a jar of oil.'

2Kings 4:2

This scripture is an excerpt from a story of the widow of a prophet who was being harassed by creditors. Because she could not pay her debts, the bill collectors were threatening to take her two sons and sell them as slaves. It was in desperation that she approached Elisha with the problem. What followed was possibly one of the best prosperity lessons ever given.

The appearance of lack indicates a need to begin giving. Like the widow, however, most of us think that when we lack, we have nothing to give. There is "nothing in the house, except a jar of oil." The jar of oil, however, is not to be underestimated. Elisha instructs the woman to go to the neighbors and borrow as many empty vessels as she can find. She is to then go into her house, close the doors and begin pouring her oil into the empty vessels. Miraculously, the oil continues to flow as long as there is another vessel ready to be filled. When the last vessel is full, the widow sells the oil, pays her debt with money to spare.

The oil, in this case, represents creative spiritual energy that is the basis of our being. No matter how convincing an appearance of lack, you and I always have a "jar of oil" in our house. Like the widow, we may think that this unassuming resource is incapable of solving our problem. Borrowing empty vessels then going into the house and shutting the door represents our going within, closing our eyes to appearances and tapping this spiritual resource in the quiet. The empty vessels represent new ideas. Filling them with oil represents charging these ideas with new energy, new enthusiasm. When the last vessel is filled, the solution is reached and the problem solved.

If we are saying, "I only have a jar of oil in the house," then we are restricting our options. If we open our mind, bring in new, empty vessels and begin pouring – affirming new possibilities – one thing leads to another and soon a solution presents itself.

It only takes one small drop of enthusiasm to spark a completely new chain of ideas, so start pouring.

When Doors Close, Minds Open

We are all familiar with the famous line from *The Sound of Music*, "When a door closes, a window opens." Many of us found inspiration in these words that offered hope in some moment of despair. How encouraging to think that when one way is blocked, another is opening.

It is equally comforting to know that the window that opens is something as close as our own mind. The door that closes represents a known path, a way, a certain state of affairs to which we have grown accustomed. Though we know the nature of life is change, when change actually occurs, when a familiar doors close we are prone to fall into bouts of fear and uncertainty as to the outcome of our future.

It is at such times that the creative aspect of the mind kicks in. In his book, *The Edinburgh Lectures*, Thomas Troward wrote,

> "The individual's subjective mind is his own innermost self, and its first care is the maintenance of the individuality of which it is the foundation."

We each have a built-in wisdom that knows how to navigate through the fog of uncertainty. It is our "innermost self," the soul, which is the direct offspring of Infinite Mind, God. Though we do not always perceive it, the soul utilizes all faculties of our mind to work immediately on new challenges that arise. We have a kind of beacon vessel traveling before us in a foggy reef, nudging us right or left to avoid the coral protrusions that lay just below the surface.

I recently met a woman whose husband, seven years ago, was killed in an accident while riding a horse. She said, "That was the darkest moment in my life." She recently met someone and a completely new life has opened for her, a life that she can only speak of through genuine tears of gratitude. She did not cling to her loss or her grief. She moved through it, and in the process, she became willing to open her mind to a completely new set of possibilities.

You may not relish this idea, but you are most alive in your moments of uncertainty. The vigor of youth rekindles in your heart. The portals of creativity reopen in your mind, allowing you to think outside the box of appearances.

If you are currently reeling from a closed door, begin now to affirm that your mind is open to new possibilities. Let go of what is past knowing that something even better is opening for you now.

The Twenty-Third Psalm Series

The Lord is My Shepherd

Part 1 of 6

The lord is my shepherd, I shall not want…

The 23rd Psalm has served as a source of comfort to millions over the years. A profound series of affirmations, this psalm reminds us there is a higher Presence working in and through us to guide us to the right thing.

The Psalmist does not say, *the lord wants to be my shepherd, and if I will love and promise to obey Him, He will take care of my wants.* He says, "The lord *is* my shepherd…" He is stating a changeless relationship that we often forget, especially in our trying moments.

A shepherd is a caretaker, a protector, one that guides his or her flock to the best and least dangerous grazing spots. Isn't this a wonderful image to hold of our relationship to God? Right now, you and I are being guided into the best and highest, the most bountiful place in life, the richest environment in which to learn and grow.

Pause for a moment to remember this. Allow yourself to let go and trust that you are in the right place at the right time, that unseen good is now unfolding through your experience. Get the feeling that you are being guided, that your unfulfilled longing is being satisfied in every way.

Affirm often: *The lord is my shepherd, I shall not want,* then listen for the quiet, gentle guidance that is calling you to trust, that is leading you to a deep, inner satisfaction. Know beyond all doubt that you are being lovingly guided through uncertain times and through territory that may be unknown to you. Nothing is unknown to God, the lord of your being, your unfailing source, your guide and your protector.

Beside Still Waters

Part 2 of 6

> He makes me lie down in green pastures. He leads me beside still waters; he restores my soul.

The imagery presented in these two lines is very calming, a wonderful visualization to begin a productive meditation time.

The Psalmist no doubt arrived at this potent visual as the result of his own experience with God. All who experience God come to know the calming, soul restoring influence of the inner light, the inner stillness, and they return to the realm of their affairs with a renewed assurance that all is well, all is in divine order.

Do you feel overwhelmed by some condition in your life? Are you in a frantic struggle to resolve it? Is there some care quietly gnawing away at your peace, perhaps interrupting your sleep or creating a distraction in your creative, more productive endeavors? Imagine yourself resting in green pastures, sitting calm and serene beside beautiful waters, feeling the restoring presence of Spirit in you imparting new strength, new inspiration and new enthusiasm from which to meet your day.

The psalmist wrote of an experience that is not only available to us all, it is our most natural state of being. A dedicated effort to return often to this inner center of quiet will cause you to realize throughout your day that *nothing can disturb the calm peace of my soul.*

When the temptation to fall into a frantic mode arises, remember the green pastures, the still waters of God's presence that restore your soul. Move into that calming, healing place, and let new light and energy lift you up to a greater sense of calm, of unwavering confidence in the greater good now unfolding through you.

The Path of Righteousness

Part 3 of 6

He leads me in paths of righteousness for his name's sake.

The Psalmist continues with the theme of spiritual guidance. The translators of the New Revised Standard Version of the Bible change the phrase, *paths of righteousness*, to *right paths*, a clarification that should prove helpful in our understanding of the idea contained in this line.

In practice, the *path of righteousness* is sometimes converted into an attitude of religious self-righteousness, one that is often condemning of those who hold beliefs incompatible with our own. The simple thought that God is leading you in right paths is a powerful, affirmative attitude that allows you to leave others to find the way that is most meaningful to them.

The word *sake* means *for the good, the benefit or the welfare of somebody or something*. In addition, Biblical names, particularly in the Old Testament, depicted a characteristic or the nature of a person or place. The phrase, *for his name's sake*, can be thought of as meaning, *for the benefit of his (God's) nature*. In other words, there is a right path for you, a way through which God seeks expression. In this line, you are affirming that God is leading you to your right path, one through which all the divine attributes of peace, health and the abundance of all good shines forth naturally.

In your times of quiet, let go of your grasping for answers. Looking outside of yourself and seeking the resolution to this or that problem is the cause of all tension of your mind, shortness of breath and stress in your body. You are on the right path when you turn to God alone for guidance. You are complying with God's nature that works from the center to the circumference of your being.

You know you are on the right path when the stress of groping for solutions subsides and the peace of God rises from your center. Affirm: *God's perfect peace is my right path and I choose this path now.* Be still. The peace of stillness is your right path.

Finding Peace in the Valley

Part 4 of 6

Even though I walk through the valley of the shadow of death, I fear no evil; for thou art with me; thy rod and thy staff, they comfort me.

I once read that the *valley of the shadow of death* was a reference to those moments when a shepherd would need to bring his flock through a narrow valley. There, predators would hide in the shadows of rocks and trees, using the narrow terrain to their advantage when they launched an attack on the flock.

Whether or not this is true, the valley here represents danger. Metaphysically, valleys represent low moments in consciousness just as mountains represent higher levels of enlightenment. We all have low moments. While we pass through them, we feel quite vulnerable to forces real and imagined that threaten to harm us or rob us of something important.

At such times, we would do well to affirm with the psalmist, *I do not fear this negative appearance. God is my protector, my refuge, my guide.* Then, we stand firm knowing the divine outworking of visible good is imminent, and we hold fast in this knowledge even when we see movement in the shadows. We affirm strength, steadfastness and courage to keep moving forward.

Shadows do strange things. The gentlest person can put a flashlight to their chin, causing shadows that make them look sinister. Move the flashlight ever so slightly and the shadows, along with their negative effect, disappear.

There will be valleys, and there will be mountaintop experiences. It is important for us to remind ourselves that God is present in them all. The 23rd Psalm is an excellent reminder of this truth.

The slightest movement of our thought toward God refreshes our faith, reassures us that life is good and that the thing you fear today is on its way out. There is peace, even in your valley of the shadow of death, and it is waiting for you now.

My Cup Overflows

Part 5 of 6

Thou preparest a table before me in the presence of my enemies; thou anointest my head with oil, my cup overflows.

Again, this line from the 23rd Psalm is rich with the ideas of protection and prosperity. The preparation of the table in the presence of enemies is a way of affirming, *Greater good is unfolding even when things appear to be working against me.*

This is a very important understanding to affirm because it is true. When your life takes an unexpected downward turn, you may react in ways that rob you of your peace and your creative optimism. The psalmist provides a key that can help you stay centered in the truth: *This thing is not as it appears. A banquet of good is set before me. I know this and I am at peace.*

Oil is a symbol of prosperity, both materially and spiritually. The head is a symbol of wisdom, intelligence. The Bible describes Joseph, for example, as "a head above his brothers," meaning, he was sharper. The image of God anointing your head with oil is a way of reminding you to open your mind to divine possibilities both of a spiritual and material nature. In times of stress, we close our minds to all but the apparent problem, and it appears that our world is falling apart. God never ceases working, anointing you with everything you need to prosper through your challenges.

The image of the cup overflowing is the most obvious. See yourself overflowing with the life, love, power and intelligence of God, touching everyone and everything that concerns you with peace, order, and an abundance of good.

Your prosperity begins from within and works its way out into your affairs. You literally overflow with divine energy. As you affirm and visualize this truth, you enhance its prospering activity in all that concerns you.

Dwelling in the House of the Lord

Part 6 of 6

> Surely goodness and mercy shall follow me all the days of my life; and I shall dwell in the house of the Lord forever.

Many of us hope to leave a legacy of "goodness and mercy," a wake of influence that touches people in positive and enlightening ways. I sense this was a desire of the author of this psalm, for he certainly accomplished it with this piece of work. I would also imagine he understood that if goodness and mercy were to follow him, he would need to strive to be good and merciful in his own daily affairs. Emerson said the same thing in a slightly different way: *If you want to be a great soul, be a great soul now.*

The first half of the last line in this famous psalm is an affirmative reminder of what is required of us if we want to make a positive, constructive impact on our world. We learn to give what we want to receive, to do unto others, as we would have them do unto us. It is not difficult to leave someone feeling better than when you found him or her. A simple kind word or act may be all it takes to turn their day for the better. The phrase, *random acts of kindness* has become a catch phrase, and yet such acts quietly performed will do more to increase your quality of life, and the quality of life for others, than you can imagine.

The more we give our light to the world, the more we realize that we already dwell in the house of the Lord. Being a conscious giver opens our eyes to things we cannot see when we are drawn in upon ourselves. The world becomes a brighter place because we bring the needed light of compassion.

Make a conscious decision today to look for ways you can sow seeds of goodness and mercy, to brighten a moment for someone, to bring optimism to the gloomy prospects that another may be facing. See your life as "the house of the Lord," full of opportunities to serve, to bless others and to be blessed in return.

End of series.

Facts versus Truth

The facts of a situation rarely represent the truth. Life is not the stagnant pool of problems it sometimes appears to be. There is always a new opening, a new idea, a different way of thinking and an inspired way of seeing things.

An Inlet and Outlet

Every man is the inlet, and may become the outlet, of all there is in God.

— Ralph Waldo Emerson

Many prominent metaphysical writers have used this insightful quote from Emerson. The idea is fitting because it portrays the individual as an integral component of a much larger context.

In the study of systems theory, this particular portrayal of the individual would be considered an open system, "a system where matter or energy can flow into and/or out of the system." There is a perpetual interaction between the part (the individual) and the whole (God). A closed system, on the other hand, is one that, in this context, would see the individual as something separate from God. This dual view of the human being also exists in science. There are those who see consciousness as a function of the brain (closed system) and those who see the brain as transmissive of non-localized consciousness (open system). This open-system view, in varying degrees, holds that human consciousness is a fully integrated aspect of a larger field that the spiritually minded would have no problem labeling God.

This open system view of the individual is one that Paul was apparently comfortable with, for he is quoted as saying, "Yet he (God) is not far from each one of us, for 'In him we live and move and have our being'" (Acts 17:27-28).

The problem confronting all people on the spiritual path lies in moving from conceptualizing our oneness with God to actually knowing that in him we truly live and move and have our being.

To enhance this awareness, I suggest using these following five affirmations from Emilie Cady in your daily times of quiet reflection. The *"You"* of course, is a reference to your indwelling Lord:

You abide within me, You are alive there now.

You are all power.

You are the fulfillment of all I desire.

Your innermost presence now radiates from the center to the circumference of my being.

I give thanks that You hear and answer me, that You now come forth into my visible world as the fulfillment of my desire.

Speak these affirmations with the calm assurance of their power to align your consciousness with the truth of your being. You are truly an inlet and may become an outlet to all there is in God.

Filling Your Life Right Where You Are

> For to everyone who has will more be given, and he will have abundance; but from him who has not, even what he has will be taken away
>
> Matthew 25:29

These words are a summary of the parable of the talents that Jesus gave. In the parable, a homeowner went on a trip and entrusted three servants with various sums of money. Two of the three invested the money and were commended by the homeowner. The third buried his portion because he feared the consequences of losing it.

The spiritual principle expressed here is to begin giving now from what you have and from where you are. Wallace D. Wattles (1860-1911), author of the classic, The Science of Getting Rich, wrote these simple words of wisdom: "Put your whole mind into present action."

Where do you want to go in life? Invest all of your being in your vision doing everything you know right now to bring it about. Do not bury your "talent" wishing, worrying, regretting or discussing how bad things are. Make every effort to start pouring your imagination, faith and your ability to act into the thing you desire. Are you in need of healing? Commit absolutely to it now. Make every mental image, every emotion conform to what you want and settle for nothing less. Do you need more money or some other form of supply? Then at this very moment, be done with your lacking image of yourself and start investing all your energy into the condition of plenty.

Do not be afraid to give from where you are. You have access to unlimited energy (talent) that can be translated into any condition you desire. Invest all your energy your desire and more will be given you in the form of new ideas, new enthusiasm and new opportunities. Don't wear yourself out looking for results. Fill your life right where you are with an absolute commitment to your desire, and it will be yours.

Forgiveness and the Art of Letting Go

The very pain that you suffer, the very failure to demonstrate over some matter that touches your own life deeply, may rest upon just this spirit of unforgiveness that you harbor toward the world in general. Put it away with resolution.

– Emilie Cady

    This statement is significant on many levels. Cady depicts the act of not forgiving as a cause for suffering, a blockage that may be keeping the greater good you desire from coming into manifestation. How could one act of holding on create an effect in a seemingly unrelated area?

    In our consideration of the spiritual principle involved, the object of our unforgiving attitude is not as relevant as the attitude itself. If someone does you wrong, for example, you will likely hold resentment toward them. Imagine a once free-flowing stream that someone blocks with sandbags. It doesn't matter why the person placed the sandbags in the stream. The drying up effect downstream is the same regardless.

We're beginning to understand that our attitudes, like the sandbags, either restrict the flow of our life or encourage it. A person you believe has done you wrong has no power to affect conditions in your life. How you think of this person does. While your motive for holding them in contempt may well be justified, you have to ask yourself if holding such an attitude is worth the inner discomfort you experience. Is it worth the potential blockage caused by your holding on to the hurt? Forgiveness is not about condoning the ill actions of another; it's about letting go of attitudes that may be blocking your good.

As a simple exercise, imagine the sandbags blocking the stream and downstream is completely dried up. With a knife, you begin slicing open the bags. The sand pours out and the water begins to move, carrying the loose sand with it. Soon the current is strong enough to wash away the sand and the empty bags.

What others do or do not do to us may have an impact, but this does not come close to the impact we have on ourselves when we refuse to let go. Apply this simple exercise to your situation and see what a difference it can make.

Focus Your Energy

> The kingdom of heaven is like treasure hidden in a field, which a man found and covered up; then in his joy he goes and sells all that he has and buys that field
>
> Matthew 13:44

The greatest treasure that you and I will ever discover is our innate ability to create the world of our choice. Doing so is a multi-level process. We first acknowledge our oneness with God's limitless energy. We form that energy into a mental and emotional image of what we want and we hold that image while creating and executing a plan of action.

In this creative process, it is important to stay focused on our objective, which is what the above parable points out. In the parable, the man sells his many possessions and buys one thing. His entire focus can then be on that one thing – the field – and extracting the treasure it contains. When we commit to a heartfelt direction in life, we must be willing to "sell" or release everything in us that goes counter to that direction. Fear, self-doubt, lethargy or ever-shifting goals are a few of the things we will release.

Think of yourself as a magnifying glass focusing sunlight to a pinpoint so powerful it can ignite a flame. Bring all the forces of your being to bear on the direction you want your life to take. If one plan seems to fail, shake the dust off your shoes and start another. Do not allow failure to become one of your possessions. Reject the thought that says *this wasn't supposed to be*. Let go of any images or feelings that run counter to what you desire, and keep moving forward. If you come to a place where you don't know what to do next, affirm, "I am open to the next step. I know what to do and I do it."

Remember the earlier lesson that once you put your hand to the plow, and then don't look back. This is another way of saying focus your energy. You have what it takes to get wherever you want to go. Embrace your ability to focus and go all the way!

Misguided Guidance

It is not unusual to hear someone complain that an answer they felt God had given them turned out wrong. In one case, after well-laid plans collapsed, I heard a woman ask, "What was God thinking?" I was told of another woman who was given a ticket for making an illegal turn into a church parking lot. She was indignant for, after all, she was going to church! How could God allow her to get a ticket for going to church? Another man was praying for his elderly mother to recover from a fall. When she passed away, he was crushed that God would let him down.

One of the reasons we struggle with such issues can be traced to our habit of laying a very human template over God, a habit which I believe the writer of Proverbs had in mind when he wrote this line:

> There is a way which seems right to a man, but its end is the way to death (Proverbs 14:12).

Of course none of the above examples were cases that ended in death to the one praying, but they certainly ended in disappointment in God's behavior. We've all experienced this. Why the flat tire on the morning of that long-awaited vacation? Why the rain on that important family picnic? Why did the person of less experience get the job I prayed for instead of me?

While most of us carry strong remnants of God as the old man in the sky that sometimes gives us what we want and other times withholds it, I believe Jesus was attempting to get his followers to think of God in a different way:

> " ... for he makes his sun rise on the evil and on the good, and sends rain on the just and on the unjust" (Matthew 5:45).

The sun does not withhold its light from those we consider evil, and rainfall is not determined by human righteousness or a lack thereof. God is life, and this life is pushing forth from center to circumference of every man, woman and child ... every living thing. This pushing forth is detected by each of us as the desire to experience greater freedom. So we latch on to certain circumstances as the means by which God delivers this gift of freedom. Spiritual freedom, however, is not found in any circumstance. We all know that today's apparent answer to prayer may very well turn out to be tomorrow's cause for prayer.

When we affirm spiritual guidance and we have a specific answer in mind, it is always wise to affirm, *This or something better.* This leaves the door open for the expression of genuine freedom through our circumstances. God does not waver in the expression department. When one thing does not work out, move on. Your desire for greater freedom is not misguided. Let this sunbeam of truth, this or something better, forever shine in your mind.

For This You Were Born

> For this I was born, and for this I have come into the world, to bear witness to the truth. Everyone who is of the truth hears my voice.
>
> John 18:37

If traditional Christian theology were accurate, you would think Jesus would have said to Pilate in this critical moment, "I'm the son of God, and I've come to take away the sins of the world." Instead, he said he had come as a witness to truth.

A witness, according to the dictionary, is somebody who gives evidence after seeing or hearing something. What Jesus saw and heard, he felt compelled to share. We have every reason to believe that he wanted to share it because he knew the joy and benefits of the truth were attainable by all who set their mind on a spiritual course.

Just as the orbiting planets indicate the presence of a central force – the sun – so your very existence indicates the presence of a central, creative force. So occupied are we with the *planets* that we have taken our eye off the truth of our invisible center. Were we aware of, and were we living our life from this energetic center, we would find the circumstances of our lives orbiting in harmony and in peace. Because we have lost sight of this central sun, our circumstances are often fraught with difficulty.

Salvation lies in becoming a witness to the truth. A witness is first an observer. As you quietly go within and observe the peace and harmony that you find there, you will notice that same peace and harmony working out through your life. Jesus indicated this was an effortless process, a yoke that was easy, a burden that was light. The difficulty lies in changing our approach to life. Before, we worked harder when problems presented themselves. Now we are learning to be still, to listen and to let go. It seems irresponsible until we understand that our letting go is the way of opening the inner floodgate for our prospering solution to emerge.

You were born to bear witness to the truth of your being. Go within often and touch that living center that will set you free.

Freedom in Divine Order

In our metaphysical teachings, we often encourage people to affirm divine order, especially when their life seems to be falling apart. Why would we suggest this? Why not take the more realistic approach to apparent disaster and deal with it for what it is?

Because affirming divine order is the realistic approach. There is no other type of order.

We are all trained to believe that there are two powers at work in our lives: the power of good and the power of evil. Evil, of course, comes in many guises, some of which we would not even necessarily label as evil. When things fall apart we may feel there is a secondary power working against us that we may not call evil, but we still think of it as a force that is contrary to our highest good.

We encourage an affirmation of divine order in the face of adversity so we can re-establish our thinking in the truth. There is only one presence and one power at work in our lives, God the good. This one power is at work even when it doesn't appear to be so. To paraphrase John, the light shines in the darkness and the darkness cannot suppress it.

Do not affirm divine order to change your circumstances to a more acceptable condition. Affirm it with the attitude that greater good is now unfolding through your life, that this condition that confronts you is the actual means through which this greater good is unfolding. You immediately perk up to new possibilities when you realize that you don't have to coax God into action, that the action of God is already in effect and is, at this very moment, coming into recognizable and prospering forms.

We must free our minds of the burden of a secondary force working against our highest good. When we establish optimism by affirming divine order, we begin to see facets of our challenges that before we could not. It may take some doing, but if we are willing to let go and trust, knowing there is only divine order, we will see the brighter side emerge from what may have looked like a very dark situation

From Place to Process

If you want to be a great soul, be a great soul now.

- Emerson

Much about the concept of spiritual guidance is a mystery to many. We often seek guidance to a place in life, a certain acquisition or a position that will empower us in our quest for fulfillment. What we seek, however, is not found in a place. What we seek is found in a process.

In truth, you and I are not empowered by things and positions. These only stir a portion of the power embodied in our spiritual nature. If you think your power comes from things and positions, then you are, as Jesus suggests, laying up for yourself treasures on earth, where moth and rust consume.

There is only one place in your life where you will ever find true empowerment and true and lasting satisfaction. That place is here and now. The point of all spiritual guidance is to bring you to this single place. What you and I are seeking in all our earthly treasures is a deep sense of satisfaction. We do not find it in our earthly treasures because satisfaction is an inner experience.

You do not need to acquire one more possession to begin the process of opening yourself to greater satisfaction. You need only begin giving fully of yourself to your life right where you are. If you are not happy with your life, then stop cursing it and start blessing it. Give yourself fully to whatever task is at hand, as if this is the most important thing in the universe. This can be everything from doing grocery shopping to taking out the trash to preparing a business proposal. Feel the satisfaction that you are bringing the fullness of your being to bear on whatever you are doing.

Spiritual evolution is a process of waking up to who and what you already are at the deepest level. The spiritual awakening is achieved by opening the gates of this deeper level in what you are doing right now, at this moment. Initiate this process, and you'll find every place is the right place.

A Better Solution

There may be a better solution to our need than the one we envision. We could be looking for a specific change in circumstances when all that is needed is a slight shift in attitude.

God Mind, Human Thinking

> Mortal mind, the term so much used and so distracting to many, is the error consciousness, which gathers its information from the outside world through the five senses. It is what Paul calls "the mind of the flesh" in contradistinction to spiritual mind; and he flatly says: "The mind of the flesh [believing what the carnal mind says] is death [sorrow, trouble, sickness]; but the mind of the Spirit [ability to still the carnal mind and let the Spirit speak within us] is life and peace.
>
> – Emilie Cady

The perspective of life that we hold is governed by our understanding of God, ourselves and the relationship we have with God. This understanding is filtered through perceptions based on input from our senses, "the mind of the flesh," and is generally limited to what seems to be true at the material level only.

God Mind is the unlimited essence of Being. Mortal mind, an archaic term, is our senses-based perception of reality. Through the process of meditation, we release our perceptions and open our mind to pure Being. As we succeed in a conscious connection with this deeper reality, our perceptions expand into alliance with God. Jesus' affirmation, "on earth as it is in heaven," is a way of saying; *let my mortal thinking become aligned with the truth of God.*

There is no separation between God and us. The perception of separation produces similar effects to actual separation. Understanding the impact our thinking has on our quality of life is an important part of developing a consciousness that is aligned with the truth of our eternal unity with God.

While many see thinking as a cause, true positive thinking is the effect of actually experiencing God. We don't think our life into a positive state; we open our inner being to our relationship of oneness with God and our thinking naturally begins to reflect the life, love, intelligence and power that God is.

How to Ask God for Help

Or what man of you, if his son asks him for bread, will give him a stone? Or if he asks for a fish, will give him a serpent? If you then, who are evil, know how to give good gifts to your children, how much more will your Father who is in heaven give good things to those who ask him!

Matthew 7:9

The spiritual principle of this passage could be stated like this: God doesn't give us things we do not ask for. So why is it that we sometimes pray for one thing and get its apparent opposite? Is God playing games, testing us like Job to see how we hold up under pressure? Might there be truth to the observation of James who suggested that prayers are not answered because we pray amiss?

A standard guitar has six strings. When all six strings are in tune, a strummed chord will produce a pleasant sound. If even one string is out of tune, you can hold the right chord and strum correctly, but the sound will be unpleasant. The sound you get is based on a predictable set of principles that will always give you the same result when you comply with the governing rules.

If we assume that Jesus is articulating a spiritual principle, then we also have to assume that our mixed results stem from our mixed asking. If you pray for a solution then rack your brain trying to come up with the answer, you have a string out of tune. If you pray for a solution expecting it to unfold in perfect order, all your strings are tuned and you synchronize yourself with the creative manifestation process.

The whole state of mind from which you ask, like the six strings of a guitar, produces a vibration that is either in tune or out of tune with the manifestation process. If you pray from a consciousness of doubt and fear, you will tend to create material conditions that support your doubts and fears. This is why Jesus said we must believe in our heart when we pray.

God does not give us things we do not ask for. Tune your whole being to the solution you seek, and it will come forth.

Roles and Purpose

It is easy to think of the many roles we play in life and associate them with our purpose for being here. We might invest so much in the role that we think of it as our purpose. The problem with doing this is that the role may end. Then what is our purpose? What if we didn't play the role so well? What if we weren't the world's best parent, or the best player on the team, or the smartest kid in the 8th grade? Will we then judge ourselves as flawed from that point on?

Whether we like it or not, as long as we have a body, we will be engaged in a variety of roles. We are a son or daughter, a mom or dad, a salesman or a housewife, a CEO or an employee. And if we're playing none of these roles, we are, at the very least, a spiritual being playing the role of a human being.

Roles change but the essence we bring to them does not. If we seek to find our purpose in the roles we play, then we are defined by the roles. We take our cues from role models. If we bring our own sense of purpose to the role, then we define the role. We bring to it an unprecedented quality that presses the role into service of the soul rather than the other way around.

You and I are not what we do. We do not want to fall into the trap of defining ourselves by our roles of age, occupation, place in family, position in society, titles, degrees, economics, or anything else in our physical history. That which we are transcends all of these roles. We will outlast every one of them.

As you move through your day, observe the many roles you play. You become the parent, the consumer, the driver, the hiker, the congregant, the board member, the artist, the person standing in the line at the post office. Pause to acknowledge, "This is not who I am. This is what I am doing right now. I am much more than what I do." Then, in that very setting, consider what this "much more" is. Who is this being, playing this particular role? Who is this being that has suddenly become conscious of playing this role?

Does this sound like a silly game? Try it. With a little practice, you may change your mind.

Singleness of Purpose

> But let him ask in faith, with no doubting, for he who doubts is like a wave of the sea that is driven and tossed by the wind. For that person must not suppose that a double-minded man, unstable in all his ways, will receive anything from the Lord.
>
> – James 1:6-8

When it comes to the demonstration of greater good in any area of your life, singleness of purpose is of the utmost importance. You achieve singleness of purpose when you bring visualization, emotion and action to bear on a given desire.

Visualization is the act of seeing your desire in complete fruition. This is much more effective than harboring a blind, indefinite hope that some good thing will somehow materialize as a remedy to your challenge. You've heard the saying, *what you see is what you get*. This is literally true when it comes to the process of visualization. What you constantly *see* with your mind's eye is what you get in the overall manifestation of your life. Make certain that you are seeing the kinds of things you want to demonstrate in your experience.

Add to your visualization the power of emotion, and you have a potent combination. *Feel* your vision. Close your eyes and see your desire. Get a clear sensation of the joy, the freedom, the opportunity that will present itself as your desired good unfolds. Investing positive emotion into your desire will bring it alive for you.

The third area – action – is a critical piece of the manifestation process. Visualization, even coupled with the power of emotion, is little more than daydreaming if there is no action to bring about your desire. As James says elsewhere, "be a doer of the word, not a hearer only." Put physical movement behind your visualization even if that movement consists simply of writing down your desire for clarity, or making a list of steps you intend to take toward bringing about your desire. Don't stop with the list making. Get busy with your plan.

Developing singleness of purpose in any direction will assure your success. Commit all the forces of your being in a given direction, and you will most assuredly arrive at the place of your desire.

The Missing Thing

> What woman, having ten silver coins, if she loses one coin, does not light a lamp and sweep the house and seek diligently until she finds it?
>
> Luke 15:8

The beginning of a new year always inspires visions of fresh possibilities, greater expressions of prosperity. It is also a time of reflection, a good time to evaluate the quality and nature of our quest for spiritual understanding.

For many, the actual spiritual quest is secondary to the material gains they envision as the result of the quest. We approach God to solve problems of health, prosperity and guidance. Upon receiving these, we are quickly off to something else, often no wiser for the acquisition. It's as if we approach the temple of God and God leaves a food basket on the steps. We are happy with the food basket, at least until it runs out. Soon we're back for another. What would happen if we actually entered the temple?

This is the missing thing in the spiritual journey of many. We are quick to snatch up the next book or rush to the new guru that promises freedom and plenty. The irony here is that the books and the teachers we love all say, "If you want to find permanent contentment, you must enter the temple." Yet we are too easily distracted to enter the inner temple that is the Source of all we seek.

The parable of the lost coin illustrates the single-minded focus required to enter the inner domain of Spirit. To "light a lamp" is to come to the realization that God is within you. To "sweep the house" is to release all preconceptions about God as the great food basket provider and seek God only for the sake of understanding. To "seek diligently until she finds it" is to stay focused until the inner light begins to dawn.

When a first-hand experience with God becomes our sole desire, our external life begins to work out in ways we would not imagine. Not only do we find the missing coin, we also get to pick up a fresh food basket on the way out of the temple.

The Personal and Transcendent Aspects of God

Many have thought of God as a personal being. The statement that God is Principle chills them, and in terror they cry out, "They have taken away my Lord, and I know not where they have laid him" (Jn. 20:13). ... God is the name we give to that unchangeable, inexorable principle at the source of all existence. To the individual consciousness God takes on personality, but as the creative underlying cause of all things, He is principle, impersonal; as expressed in each individual, He becomes personal to that one – a personal, loving, all-forgiving Father-Mother.

– Emilie Cady

In this passage, Cady addresses the age-old question of the personal and the transcendent nature of God. For some, the concept of God as a bearded old man watching over the world from a throne in the sky is comforting. Others find such imagery counter intuitive, irrational and illogical enough to debunk all of religion. Cady helps us understand God as both the universal energy and intelligence that permeates every aspect of the universe and as the personal, all-sustaining presence that numbers even the "hairs on your head."

My preference is to think of God as the creative life force, whose nature is to perpetually express more life, love, power and intelligence through all of creation and through me specifically. As such, God is my guiding, healing, prospering Source that beckons me to be still and know when I am seeking the highest and best both for myself and for others.

The universal nature of God assures that my personal thoughts and actions do not affect or change the behavior of God; they only change and affect the way I relate to God. I cannot disappoint God any more than I can disappoint the law of mathematics by insisting that 2+2=5. God, "with whom there is no variation or shadow due to change" (James 1:17) is personal and universal, a present help and an eternal support of all that I am and all that I desire to be.

The Secret of Change

> A thousand hack at the branches of evil for every one who strikes at the root.
>
> – Henry David Thoreau

One of the main reasons our life does not change in the way we envision, is that we do not confront the little self that generates unwanted conditions. As Thoreau suggests, we hack at the branches, the effects of the little self, but we leave the root untouched.

Here is a course of action that I find extremely helpful, especially when I'm experiencing moments of doubt. Deny the very existence of your fearful little self, for it has no basis in reality. That it seems real to you is not reason enough to cling to it. This little self is a product of your negative imaginings, a picture of yourself as you might be had you no supportive, underlying spiritual Source. Deny the very existence of this self and affirm that you are indeed the out-picturing of your all-embracing supportive Source. You can never be separate from your God who is manifesting freely and abundantly through you and as you now.

Any time you experience fear, anger, impatience or self-doubt, remind yourself that these emotions rise, not from your true Self but from your fearful little self. Think of this fearful little self and say:

> *You do not and cannot exist. There is absolutely no basis in reality for you. You are nothing but a shadow without substance.*

Go on to declare,

> *Only that which rises from the rich substance of God my Source, can exist. I express this shimmering new life as abundance and wholeness right now. This is what is true, and this is all that I accept.*

Self-administer this treatment several times a day, especially when you find yourself slipping into any of the negative emotions described above. This is the secret of changing conditions. Let go of the self that is creating that which you do not desire and embrace that Self from which your high vision of life arises in the first place.

The Key to Power

> And there appeared to them Eli'jah with Moses; and they were talking to Jesus. And Peter said to Jesus, 'Master, it is well that we are here; let us make three booths, one for you and one for Moses and one for Eli'jah.' For he did not know what to say, for they were exceedingly afraid. And a cloud overshadowed them, and a voice came out of the cloud, 'This is my beloved Son; listen to him.
>
> — Mark 9:4-7

This incident, known as the transfiguration, not only bears much significance in early Christian development, it also contains an important lesson for us today. The key to the early Christian's understanding of the story's meaning is found in the figures of Moses and Elijah – the Law and the Prophets. The author of Mark is telling his readers that the teachings of Jesus fulfill and even supersede those found in the Law and the Prophets. They should listen to him.

From a metaphysical point of view, Moses represents the Law as given to Israel in the past. Elijah, the prophet extraordinaire, represents the predictor of things to come, the future. Jesus represents the now. The author of Mark, in fact, prefaces the story with Jesus speaking these words: "Truly, I say to you, there are some standing here who will not taste death before they see that the kingdom of God has come with power."

The more attuned we are to this now moment, the less encumbered we are with baggage from the past and fears of an unknown future. If you feel powerless, at the mercy of forces beyond your control, chances are that you are spending a significant amount of energy looking backward or straining to see what some future horizon holds for you. The kingdom of God has come with power. You and I live in it, but this power is tucked away in the present moment and we must open our minds and hearts to it if we are to partake of its benefits.

The power you need to make right decisions is present. Affirm, *God's loving presence directs my every step. I am strong and confident that my life is unfolding in perfect order and perfect harmony. Thank You God.*

The Prospering Law of Giving

> Give, and it will be given to you; good measure, pressed down, shaken together, running over, will be put into your lap. For the measure you give will be the measure you get back.
>
> Luke 6:38

Emma Curtis Hopkins wrote, "You have but one thing to give, namely, your attention." If you apply her observation to the statement of Jesus, you begin to see why giving is an important key to the kingdom.

Your life flows where your attention goes, so the key is to begin giving your attention to the area you want to see "running over." You may be saying you want more prosperity but you are experiencing lack. If you use the guideline that the measure you give is the measure you are getting back, you will quickly see that you are giving more of your attention to lack than to prosperity. Otherwise, you would be experiencing prosperity.

Perhaps you have not grasped the truth that you are a limitless expression of the Infinite, so you are hanging on to the idea that you only have limited resources. You can determine where you are with this by observing how you feel when life suddenly nudges you out of one of your comfort zones. Do you react in ways that withdraw your power and creativity? Do you feel compelled to protect that part of you that seems threatened? While this may be the normal response, do you wish to maintain this kind of normalcy? How might a limitless expression of the Infinite respond to the same condition? Can you find some way to utilize this situation as a giver? Are there ways you can begin pouring more of yourself into this condition and make a positive difference?

We all know people who seem to drain us of our energy. We also know people who leave us feeling better than when they found us. These latter are the givers, the ones who are enjoying great returns on their gifts.

In all you do, strive to become the kind of person who leaves people and circumstances in a better condition than you found them. By so doing, you are fulfilling the prospering law of giving.

The Spiritual Context

A question was raised about why it would matter if we considered the soul as evolving or as already complete, and if batting around such ideas has practical value. The way we see ourselves at the deepest level does matter, and it does have practical value, for this is the prime determining factor in how we experience life.

One who sees him or herself as an evolving soul here to learn lessons that will advance their soul's cause, will think of their life in one way. The one who thinks of him or herself as a complete soul, here simply because they want to experience the material realm, will think of their life in another way. The first attitude is similar to taking a job strictly for the money. I don't necessarily like the job of living, but my soul is getting something out of it so I'll put up with it. The second has taken on the job of living because they actually like the work.

Placing yourself in a healthy spiritual context is one of the most important achievements you can accomplish. This, I believe, is why Jesus advised to seek first the kingdom of God and all other things would fall in place (Matthew 6:33). He was pointing out the importance of the spiritual context. If you understand who you are at the spiritual level, your material issues will fall in place. It gets no more practical than this.

We suffer because we place ourselves in a context that requires suffering. Say you don't like the job. A problem arises that is a total inconvenience, but you need the money so what can you do? You have to solve it. You put up with the job hoping someday you'll get a promotion and life will be easier.

If, on the other hand, you like your work and a problem arises, you don't solve it simply because you're being paid to do that. You solve the problem because doing so stimulates your creativity and the flow of new ideas.

The context in which you see yourself makes all the difference in how you live your life. Seek first an understanding of your true spiritual context and you will be richly rewarded.

The Thrones of Angels

> We sell the thrones of angels for a short and turbulent pleasure.
>
> Ralph Waldo Emerson

This quote from Emerson has stayed with me for many years. It reminds me of Esau, selling his birthright for a bowl of pottage. Jesus also asked what good it does to gain the world if we lose our soul in the process. We may not do anything quite as dramatic as either of these passages suggests, but if we think of the thrones of angels simply as our spiritual center, our point of strength, we see there are many ways we sell it.

The thrones of angels represent that center in us where we know our life is on track. The two most common ways we abandon our center of power is by dwelling on regrets of the past and fearing the future. In both cases we pull our point of awareness away from the only place we can take any action of consequence. This place is the now moment.

This moment is the only time we can experience our oneness with God. There is no need to resolve anything, past or present, before we avail ourselves to this point of power. We simply need to become willing to let go of whatever concerns us and turn our attention to God. Though definite answers may not come in these moments of stillness, the freedom we experience is itself an answer. Free from our struggle to resolve issues, we partake of the very peace we are seeking in our effort.

If you are selling your thrones of angels for the short and turbulent pleasure of the forceful pursuit of some resolution, let go of this pursuit. Close your eyes and relax. Remind yourself that you are an expression of God, and that the peace you seek is with you now. Stay with this simple thought until you release your tight grip on the issue and you sense that things are moving in a good direction.

Letting go is not an act of ignoring responsibilities that require our attention. It is a willingness to view these concerns from a different place. Once you touch your center of strength, you will once again take your rightful seat among the thrones of angels.

A Perceptual Lens

Our consciousness is a kind of lens through which we view everything. If we hold onto ideas that are out of integrity with the nature of the soul, we hinder the fuller expression of its true essence. Spiritual growth is the process of bringing our consciousness, the sum of our beliefs, into alignment with what is true of us at the deepest level.

Understanding Grace

One of the most famous references to the idea of grace comes from the familiar hymn, *Amazing Grace*. The hymn began its life in 1772 as part of the sermon notes of John Newton, a former English slave trader turned preacher. The last verse – "When we've been there ten thousand years …" – was added decades later by, many believe, John Rees. These lyrics were eventually set to a borrowed tune called, *New Britain*.

The first line, *Amazing grace, how sweet the sound, that saved a wretch like me,* makes total sense when you consider Newton's slave-trading history and subsequent conversion to Christianity. He undoubtedly felt that he had been spared a very long and miserable afterlife. He would have appreciated the more modern cliché, *There but for the grace of God go I*, which means that something bad that happened to others could just as easily have happened to him, were it not for God's grace.

Clearly, the idea of grace is linked to humanity's worm of the dust mentality. Webster defines grace as "unmerited divine assistance," which points to the concept of God as the moody old man who regrets having created this problem known as the human race. The grace of

God, like this limited view of God, is a product of humankind's low spiritual self-esteem.

There is no such thing as unmerited divine assistance. Jesus pointed out that the sun shines on the just and the unjust, that the prodigal son created his own suffering and that a man born blind was not stricken as a consequence of either his or his parent's sins.

God is love and love operates by law, unchanging and predictable in its nurturing behavior. Does an airplane fly by grace or because it fulfills known and predictable laws of gravity? Frankly, I would not board a plane whose flight depended on grace. I will board one that flies by law.

The concept of grace can be a major obstacle in our forward movement of developing spiritual consciousness. It is good to understand how we see our relationship to God. Do we think of ourselves, as Emerson said, as the permitted wretch, or have we embraced ourselves as expressions of the Infinite, worthy of all the support and assistance this freeing truth implies? Our answer will go a long way toward explaining why our life looks as it does.

What's in a Name?

> So out of the ground the Lord God formed every beast of the field and every bird of the air, and brought them to the man to see what he would call them; and whatever the man called every living creature, that was its name.
>
> Genesis 2:19

    This passage comes from the part in the creation story when the Lord God has created everything but the woman. Adam is given the opportunity to name things. Though this story is found in the second chapter, the incident is part of the earlier of two creation myths of Genesis. Yes, there are those who insist on taking it literally, but the real power of the story is found in the spiritual principle it illustrates. This is our power to name.

    Every time you think of something, you give it a name. You call it good, bad, challenging, something you want, something you don't want and so on. For example, let's say you awaken in the morning and remember that you have an appointment that you'd rather not attend. Immediately you name it as a thing you do not want to do. With a sigh, you wish there were some way you could get out of it, or you could get it over with and get on to other more appealing activities.

What is happening with this naming activity? As you think of this thing, you are making a decision that affects the quality of your attitude. You are saying, "I don't want this thing, so I will withhold my power from it. I will not be happy, creative and fully present as I think of this appointment." The thing becomes for you, in terms of its quality, the very name you give it.

When you first think of this appointment, try naming it something else. Name it good. Give it a name that allows you to think of it fondly. Name it something you want to experience rather than something you do not. Then allow yourself to experience the name you have given it.

The things Adam named, he declared good. Today, try following his life-enhancing example and see what a difference it makes.

When Tough Love is Called For

Of our three primary areas of concern – health, prosperity and relationships – the matter of relationships may be one of the most challenging. Most of us struggle with the fear that if we pass judgment on another, we ourselves might also experience negative repercussions of some sort. Aware of our own imperfections, we may question our right to acknowledge and challenge the potentially destructive behavior of another. There are times, however, when it is in our best interest to exercise our faculty of judgment.

Imagine an airliner carrying a group of passengers bound for a specific, mutually agreed-upon destination. In mid flight, a small group of these passengers decides that they want the airplane to go to a different destination. They notify the flight attendant of their new ideas and they demand that the captain change course. It does not matter to this small group that their fellow passengers have boarded this flight because it met their needs. Should the captain and these passengers meekly submit to the wishes of this group? Of course not.

Are the wishes of these demanding people wrong? No. Are they on the wrong flight? Apparently. Other flights will take them to their desired destination. Those who are on the flight because it meets their needs have no moral or spiritual obligation to give in to the demands of the dissenting group.

When we find ourselves in a situation involving a manipulative person who is attempting to use us to fulfill his or her own selfish ends, we are called upon to exercise tough love. We certainly want them to be on the right flight, so to speak, and we are willing to do what we can to help them make the right connection. We are under no obligation to fund their choices, change our course for their sake or meekly submit to their needs we cannot in good conscience support.

The greatest gift we can give another is to recognize that they have their own path and they have the inner resources to pursue it. They do not need to take from us anything that represents their highest good. Reminding them of this truth will likely be cast as judgmental and uncaring. Tough love is seldom popular. Still, it is the kind of love that provides the kind of incentive another may need to get on the correct flight and connect with the destination that represents their highest good.

Where is Your Heart?

Do not lay up for yourselves treasures on earth, where moth and rust consume and where thieves break in and steal, but lay up for yourselves treasures in heaven, where neither moth nor rust consumes and where thieves do not break in and steal. For where your treasure is, there will your heart be also.

Matthew 6:19-21

An important key to understanding the kingdom spoken of by Jesus is that it is spiritual, not material in nature. The material is the effect of an underlying spiritual cause. "What is seen was made out of things which do not appear" (Heb. 11:3).

To "lay up for yourselves treasures in heaven" is an instruction to build a consciousness of God as your invisible, ever-abundant source of all good, knowing this consciousness draws to us a material counterpart in the form of conditions and things.

When you pray for healing, for example, envision the reality of your present spiritual wholeness. Affirm that your wholeness is your reality that is now interacting with the atoms and cells of your physical body in ways that demonstrate wholeness. If you feel stuck in your life, quietly open your mind to the borderless reality of spirit within you, that inner energy that is even now building and sustaining worlds that have not even entered your mind. Focus on putting your being in motion in new directions. Open the floodgates of new inspiration. Don't struggle toward a different external condition. Affirm a new inner condition by seeing and feeling where you want to go emotionally.

Scriptures like this one have caused people to denounce the material realm as interference to their spiritual life. This scripture does not denounce materiality; it simply puts it in perspective. According to the gospels, Jesus manifested loaves and fishes and initiated many physical healings. He was a master of the material domain because his heart was in the all-encompassing reality of his unfailing spiritual resource.

Why Am I Here?

Not long ago, two people raised two different questions that are somewhat interwoven. One asked why are we here, what is our purpose? Another asked if I would address the issue of reincarnation. At first glance, these questions may seem unrelated, but I think you'll see that the approach I take to both issues makes them quite compatible.

For me, a good place to start is with the question of how I got here in the first place. Was I put here by God? Was I put here by my parents? Has my soul's lack of full development made it necessary for me to come here and learn lessons? While I have embraced all three of these possibilities at different times in my life, I have come to another way of thinking. In a sense, all three of these scenarios exclude the notion of free will. If God did it, I had no choice. If I am the biological product of my parents, again I had no choice. If I am here because earth life holds lessons critical to my spiritual growth, then once again, I had no choice.

Last week I made the point that life in our city means different things to different people. Some will see it as a blessing, some a curse, depending on their circumstances. Likewise, if we ask various people why they came to live in this city, we will get a variety of answers. The common denominator behind all these answers, however, is that of choice.

What if we were to declare, I am here on this earth because I made a choice to be here. While the answer of why we may have made such a choice might not be immediately apparent, the question at least puts us in a position to get an answer. If we consider the possibility of reincarnation, we can entertain the question of what keeps us coming back for more.

From a spiritual perspective, we are all here to express the life, love, power and intelligence of God in everything we do. While this may seem too abstract a notion to have any practical value, it does go along with Jesus' statement to let your light shine. By giving yourself fully to your place in life right now, by stating that you are here because this was your choice, you are letting your light shine. Your interest in the choice you made to incarnate may have changed, but your life and your place in it is still an opportunity to continue to make new choices concerning how you will let your light shine. Meditate on this possibility. Listen carefully to your intuitive response. We move through many interests, many phases but the full and responsive dynamic of life never ends. Make the choice to be here now and you may be surprised what a difference this will make.

You Just Know

> Still the intellect for the time being, and let universal Mind speak to you; and when it speaks, though it be but a "still small voice," you will know that what it says is Truth. How will you know? You will know just as you know that you are alive.
>
> – Emilie Cady

When I was very young, I remember asking my mother how I would know when I met the person with whom I could spend my life. She said, "You just know." She was right. Emilie Cady posed the same question about God and she came up with the same answer: "You will know just as you know that you are alive."

As I first began sitting in silence and turning my attention to the inner Presence, I would often experience inspirational thoughts that made me wonder if these were the "voice" of God. Over time, a new experience began to emerge that made me aware of the distinction between my thoughts, my hopes and a living essence that I knew, without question, to be a stream of life-energy from on high.

While we are looking for voices and visions, Spirit touches us in silence, when the mind is turned away from preconceived notions as to what to expect. God is Spirit, and Spirit is not a foreign substance that comes to us from afar. Even our surface preconceptions are forged from spiritual elements drawn from within, but fashioned from the directions of others. We move beyond these mental and emotional idols to that very natural, innermost sanctuary where, free from the effort of seeking, we find that which has been with us all along.

The key to finding God is in letting go of what we are expecting to find. You will not find a thundering presence. You will find a gentle, moving essence that you will know as the self-sustaining life of your being. Jesus compared it to living water which, "will become in him a spring of water welling up to eternal life" (Jn. 4:14). When Spirit touches your mind, you understand this metaphor, just as you know that you are alive

The Theory of Everything

The theory of everything is a hypothetical single, all-encompassing, coherent theoretical framework of physics that fully explains and links together all physical aspects of the universe.

Though the theory of everything is a reference to the field of physics, it is also applicable to the field of metaphysics, or spiritual matters. While science still struggles to formulate its theory, spiritually speaking we have already arrived at a conclusive, all encompassing principle that applies to every area of our life. I'm talking about the idea of the complete soul.

Whatever the problem, an experiential awareness of the soul is the answer. God, as eternal life, limitless love, boundless power and infinite intelligence, projects all of these qualities into and as our soul. If we are in need of healing, we open our mind to our spiritual wholeness and see it radiating through our body. If we are experiencing a prosperity challenge, we see the limitless energy of our boundless soul dissolving all barriers, all appearances of lack. If our need is guidance, we embrace the all-knowing mind of God fully active and guiding our every step.

It has been said, whatever the question, God is the answer. God individualizing as your soul is your ever-present help, whatever the need. Do not think of God and your soul as you would think of a genie in a lamp. Rub the lamp, the genie appears and grants your wish. Think of God and your soul as eternal, indestructible being. When you open your mind and heart to this vast, inner essence, your awareness rises from the realm of ever-changing appearances to the truth of your eternal being. Your awareness expands beyond the temporal, and you realize nothing has the power to harm you. From this point of power and strength, you move through your experience empowered by divine wisdom.

It is in stillness that you move beyond theory and come to know the peace and power you seek is already present. This knowing is the starting point of every question you have and every answer you seek.

Your Spiritual Guide

> But the Counselor, the Holy Spirit, whom the Father will send in my name, he will teach you all things, and bring to your remembrance all that I have said to you.
>
> John 14: 26

There is much written about spiritual guidance. Many seek it in scripture. Others look for it in the works of those they feel are more spiritually attuned than they. Some look for it in astrology, and still others seek instruction in the form of spirit guides.

The surest form of guidance comes, not from any outside source, but from the Holy Spirit – that is, from the wholeness of Spirit that is the very essence of your being. This Counselor, or Comforter, as King James calls it, guides, not by words or signs, but by the direct impartation of its character.

In truth, there has never been one moment in your life when guidance was absent. You may not have felt it or seen any evidence of guidance whatsoever, but it has always been there. And it is with you now.

You invoke an awareness of spiritual guidance by quietly affirming that you are now being guided. When Jesus said, "I am in the Father, and the Father is in me," he was not merely describing his unique relationship with God. He was revealing the relationship all people have with their Creator/Sustainer. "I am now in the presence of Pure Being," Charles Fillmore said, inviting all to follow him in this stimulating affirmation.

Today, affirm often: *The whole Spirit of God is the essence of my being. I move in harmony with God, and God expresses harmoniously through me.*

Bring this thought into all that you do. Feel the harmonizing, comforting presence of God in the simplest and the most complex tasks throughout your day. You are never without your Counselor, your Guide, your Comforter. Remind yourself of this often and live your life in peace.

About the Author

J Douglas Bottorff, a Unity minister for over thirty years, is the author of eight books, six nonfiction and two fiction. Doug lives with his wife, Elizabeth, in western Colorado.
Email: jdbottorff@gmail.com

Nonfiction
A Practical Guide to Meditation and Prayer
A Practical Guide to Prosperous Living
Native Soul: Unlocking Your Life's Potential
The Complete Soul: Exposing the Myth of Soul Evolution
A Spiritual Journey: An Anthology
Beams of Light

Fiction
The Whisper of Pialigos
The Way of the Bighorn

Made in United States
Orlando, FL
14 January 2024